THE *Roosevelts* *in* NEW YORK CITY

THE *Roosevelts* *in* NEW YORK CITY

BILL BLEYER

Published by The History Press
An imprint of Arcadia Publishing
Charleston, SC
www.historypress.com

Front cover, clockwise from top left: The façade of Theodore Roosevelt Birthplace National Historic Site today. *Author photo*; FDR and Eleanor leaving the East 65th Street townhouse for the White House in March 1933. *Courtesy of the Franklin D. Roosevelt Library*; The twin townhouse that Sara Delano Roosevelt had built for herself and Franklin and Eleanor Roosevelt and their children at 47 and 49 East 65th Street. The building is now Roosevelt House, owned by Hunter College. *Author photo*. Eleanor Roosevelt statue in Riverside Park. *Author photo*; A bronze sculpture of Theodore Roosevelt as he looked during a famous 1903 camping trip to Yosemite with naturalist John Muir in the Theodore Roosevelt Rotunda at the American Museum of Natural History. *Author photo*.

Back cover, inset: Roosevelt House staircase today. *Author photo*; *top*: A World War II dance at Roosevelt House. *Roosevelt House Public Policy Institute, Hunter College, CUNY*.

First published 2025

Manufactured in the United States

ISBN 9781467150309

Library of Congress Control Number: 2025936191

For Natalie Naylor, Hofstra University professor emerita, the most knowledgeable resource for Long Island history and the best manuscript editor any author could desire.

CONTENTS

ACKNOWLEDGEMENTS

Daniel Prebutt, Joseph Korber, Callie Tominsky, Ramon Mangual, Alyssa Parker Geisman and Shirley McKinney from Theodore Roosevelt Birthplace National Historic Site and the National Park Service New York City office; Clare Connelly, Laura Cinturati, Lindsay Davenport and Emily Werner of Sagamore Hill National Historic Site; Susan Sarna from the Theodore Roosevelt Presidential Library; Harold Holzer and Deborah Gardner of Roosevelt House at Hunter College; Joseph Bresnan for his help in identifying Roosevelt-related sites in Manhattan; Natalie Naylor; Howard Ehrlich of the Theodore Roosevelt Association; Christine Jacobson from Houghton Library at Harvard University; Barbara Compono, Karen Liotta, Kim Barteau, Erica Owens and Mitch Angelo of the Bayville Free Library; Joe Catalano; the late Richard Harmond, retired history professor at St. John's University; Rachel Middleton Britain of Ennead Architects; Deborah Hamer of the New Netherland Institute, Brynn White of the Century Association Archives Foundation; Janetta Lee and Declan Sokolska of the Cosmopolitan Club; Kara D.V. Avanceña at Columbia Law School; Mercedes Diez at Lehman College; Matthew C. Hanson at the Franklin D. Roosevelt Presidential Library; Brendan M. Short of the American Museum of Natural History; and the late John A. Gable, executive director of the Theodore Roosevelt Association and an encyclopedia of information about the family, who spurred me to research and write about the Roosevelts.

My reviewer/proofreaders: Natalie Naylor and Joseph Catalano for the entire manuscript and Daniel Prebutt, Joseph Korber, Harold Holzer, Deborah Gardner and Susan Sarna for selected chapters.

My History Press team: acquisition editors Banks Smither and Mike Kinsella, copy editor Abigail Fleming and publicist Maddison Potter.

INTRODUCTION

Almost four centuries ago, the progenitor of the Roosevelt family in America first set foot on Manhattan Island. From their humble beginnings with the arrival of Claes Martenszen van Rosenvelt in New Amsterdam, the Roosevelts developed into one of America's most distinguished families—one that produced two groundbreaking presidents and a first lady, as well as many other notables.

Over the years, the Roosevelts left their mark across a wide swath of New York City. From Wall Street to the Upper West Side to Roosevelt Island, there are many sites where family members lived, worked, worshipped or are commemorated by parks and statues. The most prominent of them, the re-created Theodore Roosevelt Birthplace, is operated as a museum by the National Park Service. Hunter College's Roosevelt House, initially the twin connected townhouses of Sara, Franklin and Eleanor Roosevelt, is a policy institute with many programs and exhibits open to the public.

These sites are detailed and photographed in this volume, a companion book to the author's 2016 work, *Sagamore Hill: Theodore Roosevelt's Summer White House*, and it also provides a history of the Roosevelt family in America.

1
THE EARLY ROOSEVELTS IN NEW YORK

It would take several generations for the Roosevelt family to advance to the highest ranks of New York's commercial and social hierarchy.

The first American Roosevelt, Claes (also written as Klaes) Martenszen van Rosenvelt, was described by descendant Theodore, the twenty-sixth president, as "our very common ancestor." The immigrant from Holland in the Netherlands arrived in New Amsterdam somewhere between 1644 and 1649, about two decades after a company of Dutch emigrants led by Peter Minuet first landed on Manhattan Island. Claes's name translated into English is Nicholas, son of Martin of the Field of Roses. During that period, Dutch baby boys were given a baptismal name, their father's name and a name for the location from which they came.

In historical records, the Roosevelts' surname is spelled a dozen ways, including Roosinffelt, Rosewelt and Rosvelt.[1] Robert B. Roosevelt, the twenty-sixth president's uncle, referred to within the family as RBR, even wrote a satirical letter to the *New York Sun* in 1903 to set the record straight. It was a response to a letter from Richard E. Mayne, chairman of the Department on Reading and Speech Culture of the New York State Teachers Association, who suggested that President Theodore Roosevelt was mispronouncing his last name. "The name Roosevelt is subject to over 200 variations of pronunciation," Mayne wrote. "The President pronounces his name Ro-zi-veldt….Perhaps our President does not think as deeply about the matter as academicians do." RBR responded several days later:

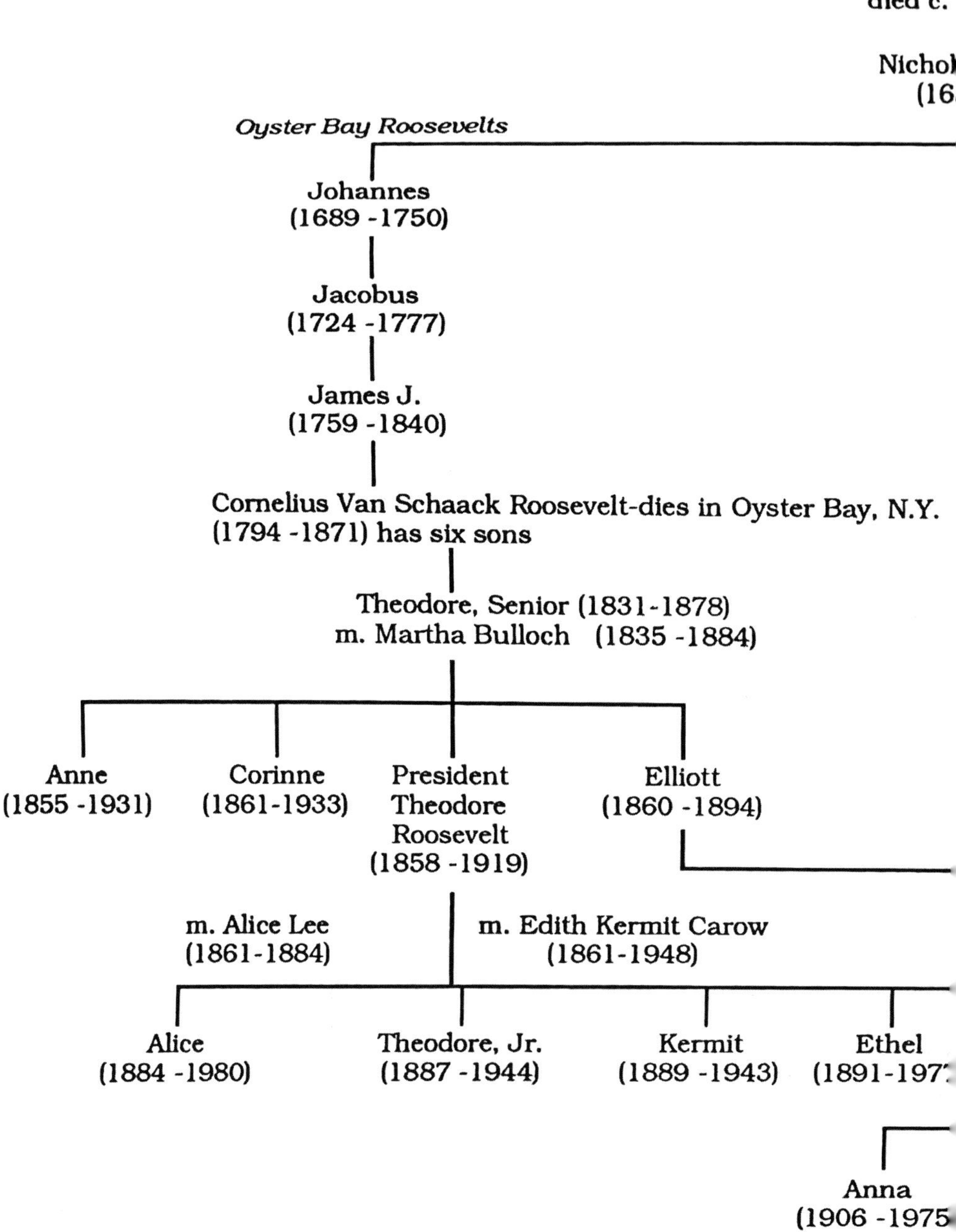

TR and *FDR* were fifth cousins.
Eleanor was *TR*'s niece. Eleanor was FDR's fifth cousin once removed.

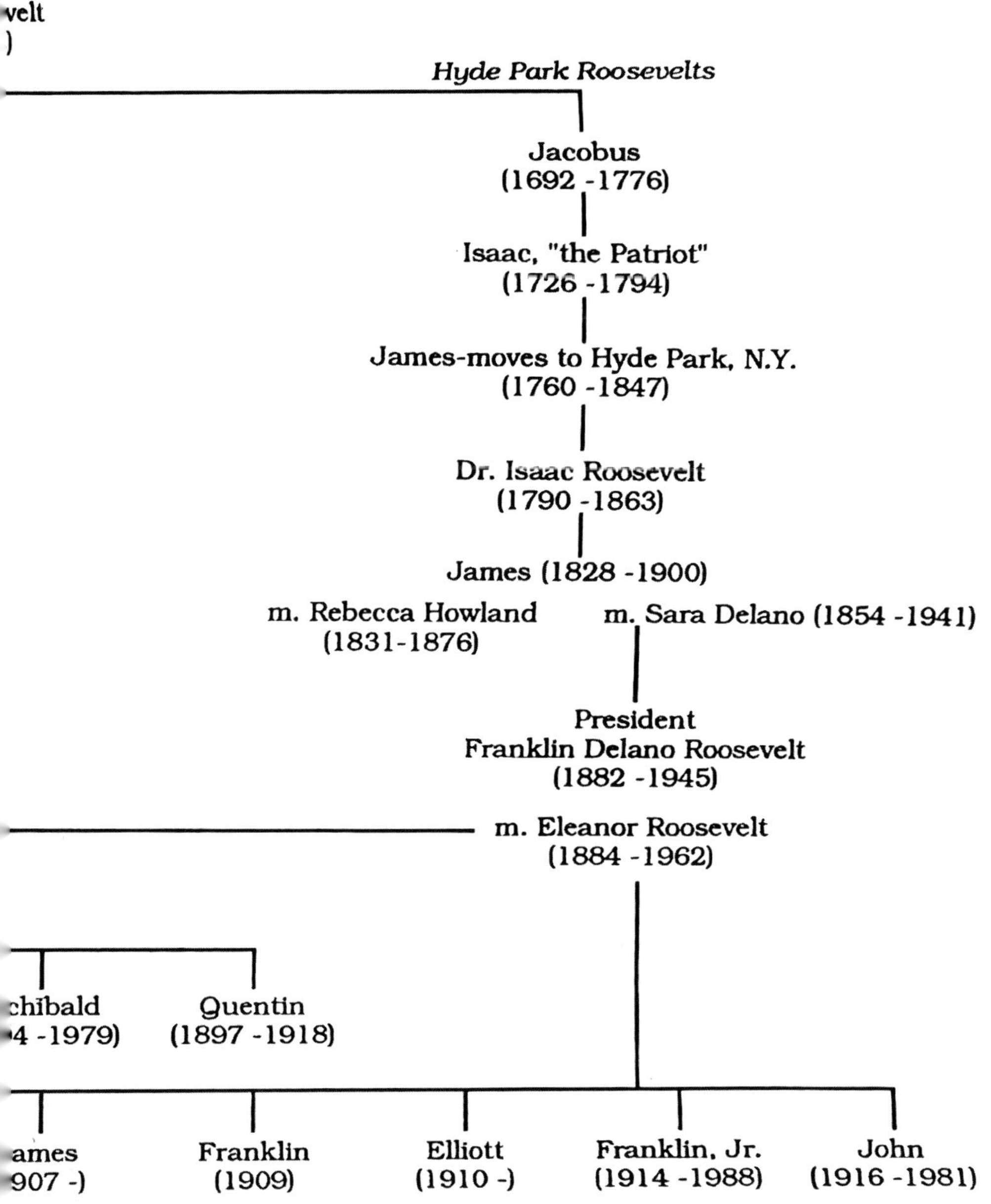

The Roosevelt family tree. *Courtesy of the Theodore Roosevelt Association.*

> *It is rather a dangerous proceeding to assume that a man does not know how to pronounce his own name, and the writer who attempts not only to criticize but to dictate may find himself in that unhappy position in which "angels fear to tread," even if he be a "chairman of reading and speech culture."…As there are readers of your paper who are justifiably anxious to know the proper pronunciation of the President's name, I will explain that it is Dutch.…The word "Roos" means* rose *and is pronounced in identically the same way under all circumstances.…The following "e"… is slightly aspirated.…So the name is "Rose-uh-veldt."*[2]

While future President Theodore was robust, the immigrant must have been diminutive in stature because his name initially appears in city records as "Cleyn Claesie," which translates as "Little Claes." To make things worse, he was burdened with the nickname of "Kleytjen," which translated as "Shorty."[3]

When Claes arrived, New Amsterdam was a tiny settlement of eight hundred people living in about eighty houses at the foot of Manhattan. Claes was a farmer with a wife named Jannetje. Claes's farm consisted of about fifty acres apparently located at today's 34th Street that he purchased from Lambert van Valckenburgh. He died sometime before 1660, when the city documents begin to refer to his children as orphans and the family name somehow changed to Roosevelt.[4]

"Who Claes Martenszen was, whether solid Dutch burgher in search of larger opportunities or solemn rogue 'two leagues ahead of the bailiff,' as his witty descendant Alice Roosevelt Longworth has suggested, is not known. In either case, by the eve of the American Revolution New York had become a bustling port city of 25,000 inhabitants, including fifty Roosevelt families. And Claes's descendants were already showing, as biographer Joseph P. Lash put it, a 'uncanny knack' of associating themselves with the forces of boom and expansion in American economic life."[5]

Claes had one son, Nicholas. As New Amsterdam was transforming into a city named New York, Nicholas as a young man headed to the northern part of the colony to work as a fur trapper in the wilderness. He returned to the city in middle age, married and fathered eight children. Nicholas built a mill near the waterfront and was elected alderman in 1700, making him the first of many Roosevelts to hold public office in America. He was also the first and only Roosevelt to be removed from office, for making "very violent and passionate expressions" against the mayor. Passionate expressions about political enemies would be a hallmark of future Roosevelts, particularly future President Theodore and his uncle Robert.[6]

"For seven generations [after Claes], Roosevelts, father and son, have from the same district in New York represented the people in the city council, the State Assembly and the United States Congress," Roosevelt biographer Thomas H. Russell wrote. Nicholas J. Roosevelt was a member of the city council in 1700–1701. His son John, a merchant and member of the council from 1748 to 1767, laid the foundation of the Roosevelt fortune. John's son Cornelius was also a merchant, elected to the council from 1785 to 1801, and his son James, another merchant, was a member of the council in 1797 at the same time as his father.[7]

Nicholas's sons Johannes, born in 1689, and Jacobus, born in 1692, accelerated the rise in the family's fortune. Johannes became a merchant and was given a monopoly to manufacture linseed oil. He also oversaw construction of many buildings in booming lower Manhattan. Johannes served on several dozen municipal committees. His house, filled with imported paintings and furnishings from Holland, was the envy of his fellow citizens. Jacobus, meanwhile, led the family into the real estate trade. This included the purchase of Beekman Swamp, adjacent to today's City Hall, for lucrative development.

Johannes was the founder of the Oyster Bay branch of the family and his brother the Hyde Park line. Before they died, the brothers Anglicized their names to John and James. Between them, they fathered twenty-two children, most of whom survived the unhealthy conditions in the city.[8]

"The pre-Revolutionary Roosevelts were prosperous burghers but not yet of the highest gentry," biographer Lash wrote. "The first Roosevelt to achieve gentility and distinction was Isaac, the great-great-great-grandfather of Franklin Delano Roosevelt, who for his services to the American cause was called 'Isaac the Patriot.'"[9]

Isaac, born in 1726, was the first Roosevelt to drop the "van" from the family surname. A trader in sugar and rum, he built a sugar refinery on Wall Street before moving to Queen Street, now known as Pearl Street, around 1772. The Roosevelt who cemented the family's fortune, Isaac by 1752 was already sufficiently prominent to have had his portrait painted by Gilbert Stuart. He also married into money. His bride was Cornelia Hoffman, whose wealthy family owned land along the Hudson River in Dutchess County, where the Hyde Park branch of the Roosevelt family would become established.

Isaac was a member of the New York Provincial Council in 1775 and helped write the state's constitution in 1777.[10] Although Isaac spent most of his time in New York City, he served in the state senate from a district around Kingston in 1777. Isaac ended his business career as president of New York's first bank, the Bank of New York, which he cofounded with his friend Alexander Hamilton. Isaac served as the state auditor for expenses incurred during the Revolution. In that role, in 1783 he approved an invoice from General George Washington for a gathering to entertain a French minister where the outlay for wine greatly exceeded the cost of the food. Diarist Philip Hone described Isaac as "proud and aristocratical."[11] Two years after the British ended their occupation in 1783, Isaac purchased property near the Bowery and First Street, a site that is now Sara D. Roosevelt Park, named after the mother of Franklin Delano Roosevelt. Isaac also owned a farm in what is now Harlem.[12]

Because of his family's wealth, Isaac and Cornelia were able to send their son James, born in 1760, as part of the fifth generation of the family in America, to the College of New Jersey, later to become Princeton University. James, who lived at 18 South Street, continued the family's success in sugar and banking.[13]

The Oyster Bay branch took longer to reach gentility and distinction. It was Isaac's cousin James who, after serving in the Continental army during the Revolution, founded Roosevelt & Son, a hardware business located at 94 Maiden Lane in today's financial district that quickly expanded into providing a wide array of building supplies.[14]

When Cornelius Van Schaack Roosevelt, great-grandson of Johannes and grandfather of President Theodore Roosevelt, took over the company, he shifted its emphasis from selling hardware to importing plate glass. The company was soon providing most of the plate glass used to build new homes in the expanding nation.

CVS, as he was known, was a short, bookish-looking man with red hair and thick glasses. He told his future wife, Margaret Barnhill, while they were courting that "the economy is my doctrine at all times at all events till I become, if it is to be so, a man of fortune." With his acute business acumen, Cornelius became the first Roosevelt millionaire.

In an interview with the author, Daniel Prebutt, the National Park Service's museum curator for Manhattan sites, described CVS as probably the shrewdest businessman of all the Roosevelts. "He knew money. He knew exactly where to be." During the Panic of 1837, CVS not only didn't panic but also invested in the future of Manhattan. "He bought up vacant lots on Manhattan Island and sat on them and waited and waited for the depression to end and the property values to come back up. And then he started selling

Roosevelt & Son, undated. *570.1. R67, Theodore Roosevelt Collection, Houghton Library, Harvard University.*

off the properties at increased value, pooled that money with some other local businessmen and formed Chemical Bank, which gave out mortgage loans. Now they're lending money to the people who are buying up these vacant lots. This is the point where the Roosevelts change from being merchants to being independently wealthy." Five years after the Panic of 1837, CVS's worth was $250,000, and three years after that his fortune had doubled. A newspaper in 1868 listed the names of Manhattan's small number of millionaires, including CVS.[15]

Cornelius Van Schaack Roosevelt. *National Park Service—Theodore Roosevelt Birthplace NHS.*

Cornelius, whose brother James I. Roosevelt had been a congressman before being appointed to New York's highest court, left Columbia College before graduation, deciding that a college education for young men going into business was unnecessary. Of CVS's five sons, Weir, the oldest, did attend Columbia College to study law, which was acceptable to his father. Robert studied law without going to college, a route available at the time for admission to the bar.[16]

Like the Roosevelts before him, Cornelius presided over a fairly sedentary family. The *New York World* noted that "the Roosevelts stock has always been noted for a tendency…to cling to the fixed and the venerable." As biographer David McCullough wrote:

> *Seldom had any of them ventured beyond the confines of Manhattan Island for reasons other than business, and never longer than necessary. They had lived and applied their renowned family acumen, met and married their Dutch wives, bred, prospered, and died, generation after generation, all within a radius of about three miles….A move from one Manhattan address to another was as serious a disruption of the pattern as a true Roosevelt cared to suffer in a lifetime. CVS had been born in Maiden Lane; the family business had been located in Maiden Lane since 1797. When, in the 1830s, CVS at last succumbed to the tide of fashion and built the house on Union Square, at 14th Street and Broadway, he did so with a consoling thought that by going that far*

uptown he had at least relieved his progeny for several generations from ever having to move again.[17]

When Cornelius married Margaret Barnhill of Philadelphia, it was an anomaly. She was the first non-Dutch person to marry into the family. Margaret was an English-Irish Quaker and the first of the Roosevelts to preach that great wealth brought social obligations to help the community and others.

But other family traditions remained unchanged. At the couple's stately Union Square home on the southwest corner of 14th Street and Broadway, the family still spoke Dutch at dinner. President Theodore Roosevelt's older sister Bamie remembered going to visit her grandparents' house with its cavernous front hall of polished black-and-white marble and great mahogany doors with silver knobs and hinges leading to the dining room. She recalled that a coal fire was always burning in the fireplace between two south-facing windows and Margaret could always be found there with her workbasket on the table and some books nearby.[18]

In *An Autobiography*, Theodore Roosevelt (TR) also wrote about his grandparents' house. "Inside, there was a large hall running up to the roof; there was a tessellated black and white marble floor, and a circular staircase round the sides of the hall, from the top floor down. We children much admired both the tessellated floor and the circular staircase."[19]

Theodore Roosevelt Sr. *Courtesy of Sagamore Hill National Historic Site, National Park Service, Oyster Bay, NY.*

TR's *Autobiography* also included an amusing anecdote about his grandfather at a young age. He said that after enduring a long Dutch Reformed church sermon for the second time on one Sunday, CVS ran toward home before the congregation dispersed. He came upon a drove of pigs on the street and mounted a large one that carried him back through the astonished and outraged churchgoers.[20]

Cornelius and Margaret had five sons, of which Theodore Sr., father of the future president, was the youngest. He would later tell his children how mortifying it had been to have to wear clothes handed down from his older brothers.

CVS was deeply interested in charitable causes and gave generously, a trait Theodore Sr. would emulate. The Roosevelt family was one of the best examples of the moneyed old Dutch families known as Knickerbockers. The family always had servants. One night, when one of the cooks got drunk, CVS went to learn what the fuss was all about; it was the first time he had ever set foot in his own kitchen.[21]

The tremendous wealth acquired by CVS meant "Theodore Sr. didn't have to work for the family business," Prebutt said. "He had enough income from the family that he could pursue a more noble effort, which again was within the Quaker mindset of fundraising and philanthropy, particularly in his case for the benefit of children and people that couldn't help themselves. So they went from being merchants to independently wealthy to fundraisers and philanthropists."

When CVS died at age seventy-seven on July 17, 1871, at Oyster Bay, where he had established a summer colony thirty-four miles east on the North Shore of Long Island, he left as much as $10 million (more than $200 million in today's money) to his four surviving sons. It was the largest fortune ever probated in Manhattan.[22]

With little enthusiasm or interest, Theodore Sr. had joined the family business not long before CVS announced his retirement and another brother, James Alfred, was elevated to senior partner. All of the Roosevelts agreed James had the best head for business in the family. Like his father, James became a director of Chemical Bank and continued the family's emphasis on banking and real estate.[23]

Biographer Lash summed up the family's status in the late 1800s:

> *By the beginning of the 20th century the Roosevelt family was one of the oldest and most distinguished in the United States. Its men had married well (including into the Howland family that had come over on the* Mayflower*). The Hudson River Roosevelts led the leisurely life of country squires and Johannes's clan was building its country houses, stables, and tennis courts along the north shore of Long Island.... Conscious of having played their part in the transformation of New York from a frail Dutch outpost into a cosmopolitan city and of the country from a handful of seaboard colonies into a continent-spanning imperial republic, the Roosevelts had a firm sense of their roots. While most of them had changed their church affiliation from Dutch Reform to Protestant Episcopal, they remained faithful churchgoers and believers in the Protestant ethic, which sanctified a ruthless competitive individualism on the one hand and, on the other, the love and charity that*

> *were the basis of the family's strong sense of social obligation.... They went on to become bankers, sportsmen, financiers, and, in two cases, president of the United States.*[24]

One of them, Theodore Roosevelt, who became the twenty-sixth president, grew up in a brownstone on East 20th Street whose story is told in the next chapter.

2

THEODORE ROOSEVELT SR.'S WEDDING PRESENT

As his father had in marrying a Quaker from Philadelphia who was not of Dutch heritage, Theodore Roosevelt Sr. broke with family tradition. The father of the future president would leave the family plate glass and banking business to focus on philanthropy, and he also would leave the Dutch Reformed Church to become a Presbyterian, the religion of his wife's family.

But Theodore Sr.'s biggest departure from previous generations was his choice of bride. He not only abandoned the pattern of marrying within the local Dutch community as his father had done, but he found his mate much farther south as well. He married a southern belle, Martha "Mittie" Bulloch, on December 22, 1853, at her family home, Bulloch Hall, in what developed into the community of Roswell, Georgia. Mittie was a beautiful, intelligent and lively eighteen-year-old member of a wealthy slaveholding plantation family who ultimately proved to be mentally and physically fragile.

The Bullochs, whom the twenty-sixth president would idolize as a child, traced their lineage to Scotland. TR described them as much more "spirited" than the Roosevelts. The first Bulloch to reach America was James, a scholar from Glasgow who landed at Charleston, South Carolina, about 1729. He became a planter active in colony politics before moving to coastal Georgia, where he had received the grant of several thousand acres. He married Jean Stobo, also of Glasgow, daughter of Archibald Stobo, a prominent figure in the Presbyterian Church who had come to Charleston in 1699.

Mittie had a sister, Anna, and a brother, Irvine, who became an officer in the Confederate navy during the Civil War and served on the commerce raiders CSS *Alabama* and CSS *Shenandoah*. Their mother, Martha Stuart Elliott Bulloch, had given Theodore Sr. her blessing for the marriage.[25]

Cornelius Van Schaack Roosevelt provided each of his five sons a house when they married. CVS offered his youngest son a house on East 20th Street in the Gramercy Park neighborhood. It was next door to the identical house gifted to Theodore's two-year-older brother, Robert Barnwell Roosevelt.

"My understanding is the brownstones were built as part of a row brownstone development—very common in Manhattan and the City of Brooklyn—where a developer would purchase a city block of land and build identical brownstones from avenue to avenue, as on East 20th Street," Daniel Prebutt, the National Park Service's museum curator for Manhattan sites, told the author. "The homes were completed in 1848, but CVS didn't purchase them until 1850, possibly getting a discount for two homes lingering on the market for two years, and holding them as presents until Theodore and Robert were married."

When the newlywed Theodore and Mittie arrived in New York early in 1854, they first lived at CVS's residence on Union Square at the southwest

Lantern slide of Theodore Roosevelt Sr. and his wife, Mittie. *National Park Service—Theodore Roosevelt Birthplace NHS.*

Above: Pencil sketch of Robert B. Roosevelt's house at 26 East 20th Street. *Theodore Roosevelt Collection Photographs: Childhood and Youth, 1858–1880. Theodore Roosevelt Collection, Harvard College Library 560.11-001c.*

Opposite: Sketch of East 20th Street. *National Park Service—Theodore Roosevelt Birthplace NHS.*

corner of Broadway and 14th Street. But within a few weeks, the couple moved into their new home, where they would live for two decades.

The brownstone façade of CVS's wedding present was a design then coming into vogue to replace the red brick of earlier upscale homes on lower Broadway and around Washington Square. The three-story house was modest compared to CVS's home with its black-and-white marble floor and circular staircases along the interior side of the building. A fourth floor was added sometime after 1865, according to National Park Service Ranger Joseph Korber. The house had initially been numbered 33 East 20th Street but was renumbered 28 East 20th in 1867.[26]

Theodore Roosevelt biographer David McCullough described the house as appearing

> *like any other New York brownstone, a narrow-fronted, sober building wholly devoid of those architectural niceties (marble sills, fanlights) that enliven the red-brick houses of an earlier era downtown. The standard high stoop with cast-iron railings approached a tall front door at the second-*

Above: Entrance hall at Theodore Roosevelt Birthplace. *National Park Service—Theodore Roosevelt Birthplace NHS.*

Opposite: Parlor in reconstructed Theodore Roosevelt Birthplace around 1923. *National Park Service—Theodore Roosevelt Birthplace NHS.*

floor level, the ground floor being the standard English basement, with its servants' entrance. A formal parlor (cut-glass chandelier, round-arched marble fireplace, piano) opened onto a long, narrow hall, as did a parlor or "library," this a windowless room remembered for its stale air and look of "gloomy respectability."[27]

The dining room was at the rear of the first floor in keeping with the standard layout. The master bedroom and nursery were on the second floor, with three more bedrooms on the floor above and the servants' quarters on the top floor.

"When the house was originally constructed," Prebutt explained, "it did not have a porch or piazza on the second floor. There were three bedrooms, and the center one was windowless. When the Roosevelts had a family, they knocked out the wall on the rear bedroom facing the alley and moved the wall in so there could be a porch out there and then put a window in the center bedroom."

The piazza overlooked yards in the neighborhood. These included that of the Goelet mansion on 19th Street, one of the largest private gardens in Manhattan and inhabited by exotic birds with clipped wings. "Daily, in their 'piazza clothes,' the children were put out to play or, in Bamie's case, in early childhood, to lie on a sofa," McCullough wrote.[28]

TR wrote that the house on East 20th Street was furnished with "canonical taste….The black haircloth furniture in the dining room scratched the bare legs of the children when they sat on it. The middle room was a library, with tables, chairs, and bookcases of gloomy respectability. It was without windows" and only used at night. "The front room, the parlor, seemed to us children to be a room of much splendor, but was open for general use only on Sunday evening or on rare occasions when there were parties. The Sunday evening family gathering was the redeeming feature in a day which otherwise we children did not enjoy—chiefly because we were all of us made to wear clean clothes and keep neat."[29]

"There were chandeliers in the parlor that were gaslit," Prebutt said. "The pendants were prisms, so when the gaslight would flicker you would have rainbows coming through the prisms. Theodore was quite obsessed with that as a child and apparently climbed up somehow and removed one of the pendants and kept it under his pillow for two days and he would play around with the prism. Then his mother noticed that the pendant was missing and you had the George Washington moment where he says, 'Well, I cannot tell a lie. I took the pendant. It's under my pillow.'"

Once settled into their new home, Theodore and Mittie assumed their place as natural leaders of the city's social and cultural scene with his family's long history in Manhattan. "New York Society modeled itself consciously on British aristocracy," Roosevelt biographer Joseph P. Lash wrote. "The elder Theodore Roosevelts…belonged to the oldest of old New York. Their name and station earned them privilege and imposed strict duties."[30]

"Theodore was invariably upright, conservative, the very model of self-control," David McCullough wrote. "He cared nothing for public acclaim. Theodore was the model duty-bound husband and father." A junior partner at Roosevelt & Son, he was a faithful communicant at the Madison Square Presbyterian Church who often attended two services on Sunday. Theodore served on charitable boards and raised money for museums. He belonged to the Union League Club and the Century Association. "Not in seven generations on the island of Manhattan had the Roosevelts produced so sturdy or so winsome an example of upper-class probity, or so fine a figure of a man—physically imposing, athletic, with China-blue eyes, chestnut hair and beard and a good, square Dutch jaw."[31]

While Theodore Sr. may have eschewed public acclaim, that did not diminish his enjoyment of the family's growing affluence. He drove coaches led by four horses through the city. Very concerned about making a good appearance, he wore the best tailored clothing and ate lavish meals at the best restaurants. He was not musical like his wife and did not share her interest in art. While he did enjoy books, he was not considered an intellectual. Theodore habitually deferred to his wife on issues of taste; he would not even buy a bottle of wine without conferring with Mittie. It was only in equine matters that he considered himself an authority.[32]

Mittie, Joseph Lash wrote, "was a flirtatious southern belle whose dark hair glowed and whose complexion seemed like moonlight. A vivacious hostess, a spirited and daring horsewoman, she made as lively an impression on New York society as she had on the ante-bellum Savannah society of the early fifties."[33]

Theodore and Mittie's first child, Anna, was born on January 7, 1855. Her parents called her Bamie, rhyming with "Sammy," short for *bambina*. Her siblings, nieces and nephews called her Bye. She painfully endured what the family called "spinal trouble" from infancy, supposedly because a nurse had dropped her.[34]

It had been difficult for Mittie to be separated from her sister and mother when she married. But they were reunited within a year because of the Bulloch family's financial difficulties. The family had to sell four slaves to pay for Mittie's wedding. To lessen the burden and help Mittie as the birth of her second child neared, Anna and her mother came north to live—initially just temporarily—at East 20th Street in 1856. "Grandmother Bulloch cared for everyone's well-being, especially her 'poor feeble child,' Mittie," biographer Kathleen Dalton wrote.

The birth of Theodore Roosevelt Jr., the couple's first son and the future president, on October 27, 1858, came after a difficult delivery by Mittie. Despite record cold and the baby being due soon, she decided to go shopping that day. On returning home, she felt unwell. Her mother dispatched servants to find a doctor, and one named Marko responded. As her condition worsened during the evening, she gave birth at 7:45 p.m. Theodore Jr.'s grandmother described him "as sweet and pretty a young baby as I had ever seen." But beautiful Mittie described him, probably at least partially facetiously, as "hideous" and looking like a terrapin. Mittie did not come downstairs until December, suggesting she was suffering from postpartum depression. Teedie (pronounced "T.D."), as the family called him, was a sickly child.[35]

Martha Bulloch wanted to return home to Georgia two months after Theodore was born, but Mittie cried every time her mother mentioned it. So Martha and Anna agreed to stay permanently. The arrangement called for Anna to serve as governess for Mittie and Theodore's children in return for room and board.[36]

Theodore Roosevelt at about age two. *Theodore Roosevelt Collection Photographs: Childhood and Youth, 1858–1880. Theodore Roosevelt Collection, Harvard College Library 10292185.*

Elliott, born in February 1860, a year and four months after Theodore, was nicknamed Ellie or Nell. In September of the following year, Corinne, nicknamed Connie, rounded out the family a year and seven months after the arrival of Elliott. All four children were born in the front bedroom over the parlor.

"During the height of population within the house, you had four children, two parents, one aunt and Grandma Bullock who came up from Roswell," Prebutt said. "But there's two bedrooms. Right around when Theodore was born as the second child, Theodore Sr. and his brother Robert agreed to raise the level of both homes by one floor to provide three additional bedrooms in each house. Bamie went upstairs and Theodore was in the nursery. When Elliott came along, Theodore went upstairs and took one of the rooms. When Corinne came along, Elliott went upstairs."

The servants came during the day and did not sleep in the house unless they worked late. There were usually four to five, including a cook and a maid. Little information is available about the employees except for Dora Watkins, an Irish nursemaid who had been hired before the Civil War. There was another Irish girl named Mary Ann, but her last name was never recorded. There was a rotation of cooks, valets, coachmen and housemaids whose names also have not been noted.[37]

Mittie, who had developed a habit of feigning sickness to gain her mother's attention, experienced increasingly deteriorated health after each birth, making her more dependent on her mother. Mittie experienced frequent digestive disorders, heart palpitations, various pains and nervous disorders. When her children gathered around her sickbed, Mittie would fascinate them with romantic tales of chivalry and the military exploits of her southern relatives or life with the family's slaves in Georgia.

Elliott was the best looking and most convivial of the four children. He was bigger than his frail and timid brother, a better athlete, and considered very kind. When he was seven, he went off for a walk with a new overcoat, and when he came home without it, he explained he had given it to a ragged child who had no coat and looked cold.[38]

The Roosevelt children were convinced they inherited their zest for life and love of people from their father. Theodore Sr. was a clear departure from his predecessors, Lash wrote.

> *The male Roosevelts were solid, industrious, worthy Dutch burghers, and also in the Dutch tradition—they were a humorless, sober sided lot. Theodore Senior, who belonged to the seventh generation of American Roosevelts, was also blessed with vivacity and tenderness, and in him there began to emerge that special blend of grace, vitality, courage, and responsibility that is called charisma and that his contemporaries found irresistible. A big, powerful, bearded man, he moved easily and comfortably in the worlds of Knickerbocker society, business, philanthropy, and civic enterprise.*[39]

Theodore Roosevelt at about age four. *Theodore Roosevelt Collection Photographs: Childhood and Youth, 1858–1880. Theodore Roosevelt Collection, Harvard College Library 520.11-003.*

"My father stands out as the most dominant figure in our early childhood," Corinne Roosevelt Robinson later wrote. "Not that my mother was not equally individual, but her delicate health prevented her from entering into our sports and unruly doings as our father did."[40]

TR idolized his father, writing that "we children adored him." He added that Theodore Sr. was the only man of whom he had ever been truly afraid. TR meant that he feared disappointing his father, although Theodore Sr. did once administer corporal punishment when Teedie was four years old and bit Bamie. Theodore wrote in *An Autobiography*,

> *I do not remember biting her arm, but I do remember running down to the yard, perfectly conscious that I had committed a crime. From the yard I went into the kitchen, got some dough*

> *from the cook, and crawled under the kitchen table. In a minute or two my father entered from the yard and asked where I was. The warmhearted Irish cook had a characteristic contempt for "informers," but although she said nothing she compromised between informing and her conscience by casting a look under the table. My father immediately dropped on all fours and darted for me. I feebly heaved the dough at him, and, having the advantage of him because I could stand up under the table, got a fair start for the stairs, but was caught halfway up them. The punishment that ensued fitted the crime, and I hope—and believe—that it did me some good.*[41]

Young Theodore was described as a loving child of unlimited energy and brightness. But as the biting incident illustrates, sometimes his energy and rambunctious nature could be trying for the adults in the household. Mittie warned her husband that "Teedie is the most affectionate and endearing little creature in his ways, but begins to require his father's discipline rather sadly. He is brimming full of mischief and has to be watched all the time." His grandmother described him as "a mischievous little rogue."[42]

3
LIFE AT 28 EAST 20TH STREET

Theodore and Mittie Roosevelt's four children grew up in relative isolation. They were mostly homeschooled. No one from the Roosevelts' social circle sent their children to public schools, and the four children had little experience with private schools because of their parents' concerns about their health. Their aunt Anna tutored them at home until she married James K. Gracie in 1866, when she was succeeded by other tutors. His Aunt Anna "was as devoted to us children as was my mother herself, and we were equally devoted to her in return," Theodore would later write. "She taught us our lessons while we were little. She and my mother used to entertain us by the hour with tales of life on the Georgia plantations."[43] Much of what they learned came from Theodore Sr., who discussed authors and had them recite poetry.

"I never went to the public schools," TR later wrote. "For a few months I attended Professor McMullen's school in Twentieth Street near the house where I was born, but most of the time I had tutors….My aunt taught me when I was small….At one time we had a French governess, a loved and valued 'mam'selle,' in the household."[44]

The most prominent tutor was Arthur Cutler, who helped Theodore Jr. prepare for Harvard and who later founded the Cutler School in Manhattan.[45] Cutler was a young Harvard College graduate hired in 1874 to tutor Theodore, Elliott and Connie as well as West Roosevelt, son of Theodore Sr.'s late brother Weir. Initially, the four youngsters studied at the same pace, but quickly Teedie, who was spending between six and eight hours a day on his formal education, pulled ahead. At that point, it was determined that he would likely be going to college while Ellie would not. So Cutler focused his time with Teedie on working to pass the entrance examination for Harvard, chosen likely for its prestige and preeminence in natural science study.[46]

The lack of schooling outside the home isolated the children, whose playmates primarily were their cousins and children of a few old family friends. There is no record of Bamie having any childhood friends, while the three younger children had only one significant friend, Edith Carow, who was the same age as Corinne and would eventually become TR's second wife. A student at Miss Comstock's School, she was the daughter of Charles Carow, a longtime friend of Theodore Sr. whose business losses turned him into an alcoholic. Edith was also tutored in the Roosevelt household when she was young.[47]

Theodore Roosevelt at about age six or seven. *Theodore Roosevelt Collection Photographs: Childhood and Youth, 1858–1880. Theodore Roosevelt Collection, Harvard College Library 520.11-004.*

The Civil War

The Civil War divided the Roosevelt household as it divided the nation. "The Confederacy was a living presence in the Roosevelt household," Lash wrote. Mittie, her sister Anna and Grandma Bulloch "did not hide their passionate southern loyalties."[48]

At the urging of his wife, whose brother and other relatives served the Confederacy, Theodore Sr., who was twenty-nine when the conflict erupted, did not enlist to fight for the Union. Instead, he joined a "home guard" cavalry unit formed to protect New York City against Confederate incursions. And as allowed under the nation's first draft law passed in 1863, he paid for one or two substitutes—possibly as much as $1,000—to fight in his place and instead supported the cause as a civilian. It was a decision that haunted Theodore Sr. and forever rankled his son Theodore. In an unpublished manuscript in the collection of the Houghton Library at Harvard University, daughter Bamie said her father felt shame for the rest of his life that "he had done a very wrong thing in not having put every other feeling aside and joined the absolute fighting forces." Theodore's brother Robert next door and his wife, Elizabeth, also disagreed about participation in the war effort. Robert also did not enlist and joined a New York State militia unit.[49]

After deciding not to fight, Theodore Sr. helped organize the U.S. Sanitary Commission, which provided medical assistance to the army. He joined enthusiastically in founding the Union League Club, whose purpose was to support the war effort. As a member of its executive committee, he aided in raising and equipping some of the first Black regiments in the war after that was allowed by President Abraham Lincoln's Emancipation Proclamation issued on January 1, 1863.

After Theodore's death, his friend William E. Dodge wrote in a memorial for a meeting of the club in February 1878 that "he felt that the withdrawal from the homes of so many enlisted men would leave great want in many sections of the country." So Theodore helped draft a bill to appoint volunteer allotment commissioners who would work with the War Department to arrange for soldiers to send home part of their pay that they did not need in their camps. For three months, Theodore and others "worked in Washington to secure passage of this act—delayed by the utter inability of Congressmen to understand why anyone should urge a bill from which no one could selfishly secure advantage," Dodge continued. It took a year to draft the Federal Allotment Law, have Theodore obtain President Lincoln's approval and get it passed by Congress. After Theodore was appointed by Lincoln as one of the three commissioners for New York State, he spent another year visiting regiments to persuade soldiers to take advantage of the allotment system. The New York State Allotment Commission saved more than $5 million in pay for the state's soldiers at no cost to them. Theodore spent thirty-one nights sleeping on trains in a two-month period generating support for the allotment system in upstate New York. During his travels, he was injured in a railroad accident and then nearly died of typhoid fever.[50] Ultimately, Dodge wrote, Theodore's efforts "resulted in sending many millions of dollars to homes where it was greatly needed, kept the memory of wives and children fresh in the minds of the soldiers, and greatly improved their morale. Other States followed, and the economical results were very great."

Dodge added that toward the end of the war, "finding the crippled soldiers and their families of those who had fallen were suffering from back pay due and for pensions, and that a race of greedy and wicked men were taking advantage of their needs to plunder them, he joined in organizing the Protective War-Claim Association, which without charge collected these dues. This saved to the soldiers' families more than $1,000,000 of fees." Theodore also created a Soldiers Employment

Abraham Lincoln's New York funeral procession in 1865. Theodore and Elliott Roosevelt are visible in the window of their grandfather's house on Union Square in the upper left. *570.1.R67c, Theodore Roosevelt Collection, Houghton Library, Harvard University.*

Bureau to find jobs for crippled veterans who by the loss of a limb could no longer work in their previous occupations. "This did wonders toward absorbing into the population of the country those who otherwise would have been dependent, and preserved the self-respect of the men."[51]

Meanwhile, as the war dragged on, when Theodore was away, the three Southern sympathizers living under his roof unfurled a hidden Confederate flag and put together packages of flannel shirts, woolen socks, scarves, combs, toothbrushes and soap that they sent secretly via blockade runners operating out of Nassau in the Bahamas to family and friends in Georgia. Saturday dinners at CVS's house, where support for the Union was strident, became such a trial for Mittie that she stopped going after "something occurred there which has made my blood boil," she wrote to her husband.[52]

While Theodore was away persuading soldiers to send their money home, his children took ill one after the other. In one letter, Mittie wrote that Teedie was "very unwell." While she didn't mention asthma, that may be when the disease that plagued his early years first appeared. "I was up with him six or seven times during the night," she wrote.[53]

As the war raged on into its third year, Grandmother Bulloch died in October 1864 at age sixty-five. She was buried in the Roosevelt plot in fashionable Green-Wood Cemetery across the East River in Brooklyn.

After the assassination of President Lincoln the following spring, when his New York funeral procession moved up Broadway on April 25, a photograph was taken as it passed CVS's house on Union Square. It shows the heads of two small children watching from a window on the second floor. They are believed to be Teedie, then six, and Ellie, four. Three-year-old friend Edith Carow stood briefly with Teedie and Ellie at the window of CVS's house during the procession. But when she began to cry, Teedie locked her in a closet so she would not disrupt the brothers from concentrating on the scene below. Despite that slight, Edith and TR remained close friends.[54]

POSTWAR LIFE

Even with her southern upbringing and sympathies, when the war ended Mittie again became one of the most prominent and respected women in New York City. Other women looked to her to set standards for fashion and activity. "Mittie was among the five or six gentlewomen of such birth, breeding, and tact that people were 'always satisfied to be led by them,' acknowledged Mrs. Burton Harrison, one of New York's smartest hostesses." She liked to tell stories about growing up in the South. Many were about her "little black shadow," a slave she had been given at birth. "She was, however, completely helpless when faced with the smallest everyday task. She was habitually, almost compulsively tardy, and household accounts were a mystery to her," biographer Joseph P. Lash wrote.[55] Because of Mittie's ill health and temperament, many of the tasks involved in running a household that typically would be done by a wife fell to her husband and increasingly on elder daughter Bamie. Theodore Sr. was the one who hired and fired servants and ordered coal to heat the house, ice to keep food from spoiling, food for dinner parties and medicines for the sick children. Mittie would frequently abandon her family to seek cures at stylish resorts. Sometimes she felt guilty when she escaped the household, calling herself a "deserter." But her behavior did not change. TR and Bamie would later consider their mother a prime example of malingering and helpless femininity.[56]

As Theodore's wealth from the family business increased, Mittie spent liberally. Her mother had always cautioned against ostentation in dress or furnishings. But after Martha Bulloch's death, Mittie undertook a major renovation of the house. She brightened the parlor with pale French wallpaper and reupholstered the furniture in sky-blue damask.[57] While Mittie ignored taking care of the house and sometimes her children, bills still came regularly from her purchases from Tiffany's, A.T. Stewart's department store and dressmakers.[58]

Later in life, Mittie would be described as eccentric. She liked to dress in white even in winter. And she was obsessive about keeping the house, her clothes and her children clean, exhausting herself in the effort. She usually bathed twice daily. Her health was fragile, with bouts of intestinal distress that led to her being put on restricted diets by doctors. But she never complained.[59]

Even though Theodore Sr. worked at the family firm and served as president of the State Board of Charities and engaged in numerous other philanthropic activities, he made plenty of time for his family. Days at East 20th Street began with the three youngest children waiting at the foot of the long stairway for their father to come down and conduct morning prayers in the library. "There were three of us young children, and we used to sit with father on the sofa," TR wrote. "The place between father and the arm of the sofa we called the 'cubby-hole.' The child who got that place we regarded as especially favored both in comfort and somehow or other in rank and title. The two who were left to sit on the much wider expanse of the sofa on the other side of father were outsiders for the time being."[60]

Later in the day or evening, TR related, he and his younger siblings "used to wait in the library in the evening until we could hear his key rattling in the latch of the front hall, and then rush out to greet him; and we would troop into his room while he was dressing, to stay there as long as we were permitted, eagerly examining anything which came out of his pockets which could be regarded as an attractive novelty."[61] Theodore Sr. kept trinkets in a little box on his dressing table, which the children always spoke of as "treasures."[62] The Roosevelts always dressed formally for dinner. When there were guests, such as Abraham Lincoln's personal secretary and future Secretary of State John Hay, the children were expected to sit quietly and pay attention to the conversation.[63]

Christmas was a favorite time for the Roosevelt children. "On Christmas Eve each child hung up the largest stocking which could be borrowed from the grown members of the family, and before dawn on Christmas morning they were all seated on their parents' bed exploring the treasures which had so miraculously arrived during the night. After breakfast the bigger Christmas presents were found in the drawing-room, each child's presents arranged on a separate table," biographer William Draper Lewis related. TR later wrote that "I never knew anyone else [to] have such attractive Christmases, and in the next generation I tried to reproduce them exactly for my own children."[64]

Theodore Sr.'s Charitable Work

While Theodore Sr. was the head of Roosevelt & Son's plate glass division, after the Civil War he devoted increasingly more of his time to philanthropy and civic enterprises until finally leaving the business altogether.

Theodore was a founder of the Metropolitan Museum of Art and the American Museum of Natural History, the charter for which was approved in the front parlor at 28 East 20th Street on April 8, 1869. He helped start the Orthopedic Hospital and contributed liberally to charities. He was particularly supportive of the Newsboys' Lodging House on West 18th Street, where every night several hundred newsboys and other stray boys could sleep in a clean bed for five cents and where Theodore Sr. led a class for poor young men.[65]

"Public concern for poverty, social welfare, and reform were something new in the elder Theodore's days," Joseph Lash wrote. "Fashionable New York, then centered on lower Fifth and Madison Avenues, was only a stone's throw from the tenements on the East Side and the squatters' shanties on the West Side, but most of the wealthy were content to keep them out of sight and out of mind." But not Theodore Sr. "He was not content to serve on boards; he needed to be actively involved with those he sought to help."[66]

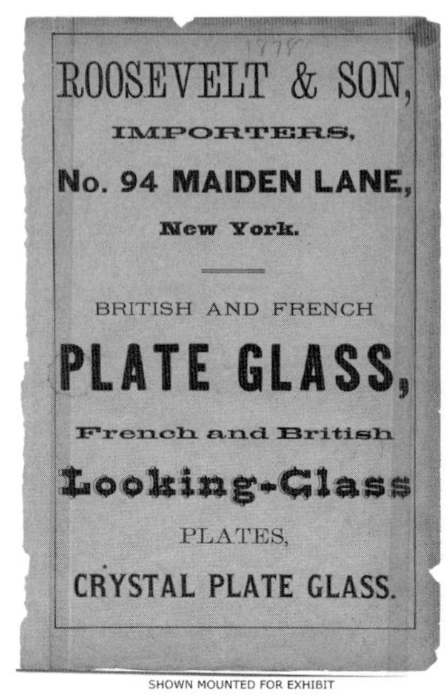

An advertisement for Roosevelt & Son. *National Park Service—Theodore Roosevelt Birthplace NHS.*

"My brother's great love for his humankind was a direct inheritance from the man who was one of the founders in his city of nearly every patriotic, humanitarian, and educational endeavor," TR's sister Corinne Roosevelt Robinson later wrote. "I think, perhaps, the combination of the stern old Dutch blood with the Irish blood...made my father what he was—unswerving in duty, impeccable in honesty and uprightness, and yet responsive to the joy of life to such an extent that he would dance all night, and drive his 'four-in-hand' coach so fast that the old tradition was that his grooms frequently fell out at the corners."[67]

"He did the most extraordinary amount of active organizational work, being one of the founders of the Children's Aid Society, of the State Aid Society, of the Sanitary Commission and Allotment Commission in the time of the Civil War, and of the Orthopaedic Hospital, not to mention the Museum of Natural History and the Museum of Art," Corinne wrote. But it was not enough for him to be active on the organizational level. He needed to be connected to his causes on a personal level. "I remember that he always gave up one day of every week (and he was a very busy merchant and then banker) to the personal visiting of the poor in their homes," she added.[68]

Theodore would often stay up until two o'clock in the morning to write letters. He visited hospitals, prisons and slums while urging establishment of workhouses for vagrants. He toured the awful insane asylums on Ward's and Blackwell's Islands and then led delegations of city officials to see them. With Louisa Schuyler, another philanthropist who founded the first nursing school in the United States, he tried to bring order to all the charitable work going on the city by launching a Bureau of Charities, the first of its kind, with Theodore serving as chairman.[69]

But Theodore never let his community interests overshadow his attention to his family. "First and foremost," Lash wrote, "Theodore Sr. was a family man fully involved in the upbringing and education of his children." He worried that if health issues for Teedie, Bamie and Elliott were not corrected they would seriously limit his children's activities and futures.[70]

Bamie

Anna Roosevelt was burdened with deep-set eyes and heavy lids that made her look tired, older and not attractive. Bamie also likely suffered from Pott's disease, a form of tuberculosis that softens and destroys the bones and turns a person into a hunchback. Bamie experienced such severe curvature of the spine and intense pain that when she was three she was fitted with what she called a "terrible instrument," a heavy steel and leather brace that left her immobile and created sores on her back. A doctor came each morning to treat the sores and strap her back into the contraption. The rest of the day she had to be picked up and carried from room to room, where she could only lie face down. Finally, in the evening, her father would remove the brace and her grandmother would rub her legs until she fell asleep. Bamie's father showed unusual devotion to her, initially because of her suffering and later because she was so mature and helped run the household. At the end of the day, when he returned from the family firm, he would go directly to see her on the piazza, bringing her ice cream, fresh peaches or a small gift and then sit with her while she had supper before he would carry her to bed "in his very strong arms."[71]

Bamie was finally freed from the apparatus for good in the summer of 1859 when she was four after her father found a new doctor, Charles Fayette Taylor, an orthopedic surgeon who was considered a quack by some of his colleagues. He treated Bamie's disease with his "movement cure," a form of physical therapy he had learned in Europe. It transformed her life. Bamie also was fitted with a different kind of back brace that was much lighter. "Instead of the terrible instrument that I formerly had to wear," she said, the new one "allowed my being up and about all the time" so that she "became very strong and well."[72]

It was the slow but unmistakable progress evidenced by Bamie that led Theodore Sr. to establish an orthopedic hospital headed by Taylor. Bamie, however, was never fully cured and spent most of her childhood forced to lie down part of every day. And for the rest of her life, she wore a piece of ram's wool on her back under her clothes so she could sit comfortably in a chair.[73]

Bright, conscientious and a quick learner, Bamie learned French and how to play the piano. She had almost as much energy as her father and Teedie, but her most noticeable characteristic was her maturity for her age. Grandmother Bulloch called her "dear busy Bamie."[74] The oldest child's main preoccupation was to be useful. Her three younger siblings treated Bamie like a grown-up and surrogate parent. If Mittie was elsewhere or suffering from ill health, Bamie ran the household for her father. When he was expecting company for dinner one night, he left her a note that read: "Order it at prompt quarter before seven. Menu as usual—raw oysters if small, soup, oyster coquilles, saddle of venison if in the house, or turkey, croquettes, quail, lobster salad, cheese and crackers, candied fruit, ice cream of course. Give John [the new butler] the wines and tell him and Mary [Ann] that I wish everything nice." If Bamie had the misfortune of being homely, physically deformed and sickly, Theodore was determined to give her life purpose by being useful. Bamie excelled at that and lived for the challenge of pleasing her father.[75]

While the boys were busy exercising on the piazza, their father continued to dote on Bamie. Saturdays were their special day, and Theodore Sr. allowed nothing to interfere with them. Father and daughter would ride horses in Central Park and then visit the American Museum of Natural History, then located in the old arsenal at 64th Street and 5th Avenue, or drop in at one of the Children's Aid Society schools that Theodore supported.[76]

TEEDIE'S SICKLY CHILDHOOD

While early descriptions of Teedie demonstrate a vital and mischievous youngster, "on reading the family correspondence as a whole, one finds that the majority of references to Theodore concern his illnesses. Starting with the fall of 1861, the accounts of colds, fevers, coughs, and stomach upsets is [*sic*] continuous," biographer Carlton Putnam wrote. Corinne also suffered from asthma, but not to the extent of Teedie. "Trips, outings, summer vacations, even journeys abroad, were planned with a view to helping Theodore to breathe."[77]

"I was a sickly, delicate boy, suffered much from asthma, and frequently had to be taken away on trips to find a place where I could breathe," TR wrote in *An Autobiography*. "One of my memories is of my father walking up and down the room with me his arms at night when I was a very small person, and of sitting up in bed gasping, with my father and mother trying to help me."[78]

The terrifying attacks occurred mostly at night, and Teedie often had to sleep propped up in bed or in a big chair to get enough air into his lungs. Sometimes his father picking him up and walking the floor with him for hours did not curb an attack. Then often Theodore Sr. would bundle up his son and take him for a carriage ride in the hope that the sudden change of air and the excitement might bring relief, which it sometimes did.

"Theodore Roosevelt, whose name later became the synonym of viral health and vigor, was a fragile, patient sufferer in those early days of the nursery in 20th Street," his sister Corinne wrote. "I can see him now struggling with the effort to breathe—for his enemy was that terrible trouble, asthma—but always ready to give the turbulent 'little ones' the drink of water, book, or plaything which they vociferously demanded, or equally ready to weave for us long stories of animal life. We used to sit, Elliott and I, unto little chairs, near the higher chair which was his, and drink in these tales of endless variety." Teedie would spin out serial stories "which never flagged an interest for us, though sometimes it continued from week to week, or even from month to month."[79]

To determine the cause of Teedie's breathing problems, doctors looked at food, plants, dust, dog and cat hair and other factors, but they never came up with an answer. That raised questions about whether the cause was psychological. His parents and doctors tried all of the popular and primitive supposed remedies, including black coffee, smoking cigars, doses of ipecac medication to induce vomiting, mineral water cures at resorts, mustard plasters, vigorous deep massages and even electrical charges.[80]

Theodore Roosevelt at about age eleven. *Theodore Roosevelt Collection Photographs: Childhood and Youth, 1858–1880. Theodore Roosevelt Collection, Harvard College Library 520.11*-005.

In the spring of 1870, the Roosevelts returned from a long trip to Europe as New York City was buzzing about the start of the long-awaited construction on a bridge to connect Manhattan and Brooklyn and the city's first subway that had opened downtown. By summer, Teedie, whose health had been generally good during the trip, suffered a serious relapse. With the return of the asthma attacks, Theodore and Mittie took turns rushing him off to Oyster Bay, Saratoga and other places, often without the rest of the family. Theodore, so busy with work at the family firm and his philanthropic endeavors, was losing patience. Sometime in the fall, the father had his famous talk with Teedie, then eleven or twelve. "Theodore, you have the mind, but you have not the body, and without the help of the body the mind cannot go as far as it should," he said, according to the account given by Mittie. "You must make your body. It is hard drudgery to make one's body, but I know you will do it." Teedie said he would.[81]

The initial mechanism for Teedie's makeover was daily workouts at Wood's Gymnasium. Mittie took Teedie and Elliott there to exercise under the supervision of John Wood, who also trained young Vanderbilts and other members of society. Mittie never missed a day, sitting on a large settee against the wall dressed in white while intently watching. Teedie worked out on a weight machine, pulling weights up off the floor and then slowly lowering them repeatedly. The boys assaulted punching bags, lifted dumbbells and strained on the horizontal bars. This went on for about three months until the Roosevelts arranged for Wood to equip the back piazza on the second floor of the East 20th Street house with all of the necessary apparatus so the boys could exercise at home.

While Teedie was relentless in pursuing the workouts, initially there seemed to be little improvement in his physique and general health. He remained small, scrawny and underweight—an irresistible temptation for bullies when Elliott wasn't around to protect him. Wounded by his inability to protect himself, young Theodore persuaded his father to allow him to take boxing lessons, which were provided by a former prizefighter named John Long.[82]

In his diary, TR frequently recorded notations such as "I was sick of the asthma last night. I sat up for four successive hours and Poppa made me smoke a cigar."[83]

Teedie's Interest in Natural History

Forced to be a homebody because of his health, Teedie found an outlet in studying nature. It led to what he believed to be an early career choice around age seven or eight as he recounted in *An Autobiography*.

> *I remember distinctly the first day that I started on my career as a zoologist. I was walking up Broadway, as I passed the market to which I used to sometimes be sent before breakfast to get strawberries. I suddenly saw a dead seal laid out on a slab of wood. That seal filled me with every possible feeling of romance and adventure. I asked where it was killed, and was informed in the harbor.*

For as long as the seal remained there,

> *I haunted the neighborhood of the market day after day. I measured it, and I recall that, not having a tape measure, I had to do my best to get its girth with a folding pocket foot-rule, a difficult undertaking. I carefully made a record of the utterly useless measurements, and at once began to write a natural history of my own, on the strength of that seal. This, and subsequent natural histories, were written down in blank books in simplified spelling, wholly unpremeditated and unscientific. I had vague aspirations of in some way or another owning and preserving that seal, but they never got beyond the purely formless stage. I think, however, I did get that seal skull, and with two of my cousins promptly started what we ambitiously called the "Roosevelt Museum of Natural History."*[84]

Teedie at first kept the collection in his room "until a rebellion on the part of the chambermaid received the approval of the higher authorities of the household and the collection was moved up to a kind of bookcase in the back hall upstairs. It was the ordinary small boy's collection of curios, quite incongruous and entirely valueless except from the standpoint of the boy himself. My father and mother encouraged me warmly in this, as they always did in anything that could give me wholesome pleasure or help to develop me."[85] Teedie's museum had grown to more than one thousand items by the time he was eleven.

Not everything remained in the back hall upstairs. Dinner guests might be shocked to see a snake emerge from a water pitcher on the table. Young Theodore kept pet mice in a bureau drawer containing several hundred specimens. At one dinner, one of Teedie's pet mice[86] emerged from a hole in a block of cheese being passed around the table. When he was eight, his mother threw out two dead mice he had stored in the icebox for future study; the fledgling naturalist responded indignantly that his mother was "defeating the ends of science."[87]

Teedie's younger sister recalled that when he was seven he wrote an essay titled "The Foregoing Ant." He had read a natural history book that described various species of ants; in one passage, the author referred to an ant that he had described previously as "the foregoing ant." The young scientist, thinking this was a species of ant, decided to write about it.[88]

TR wrote later that his naturalist explorations were tempered by a physical shortcoming other than asthma. "Quite unknown to myself, I was, while a boy, under a hopeless disadvantage in studying nature. I was very nearsighted, so that the only things I could study were those I ran against or stumbled over."[89] But the problem would not be recognized or resolved immediately by his parents.

Teedie's first experience with wilderness came in the summer of 1871, which was marked by the death of his paternal grandfather, Cornelius Van Schaack Roosevelt. Theodore Sr. organized an expedition to the Adirondacks. By now, TR was using the proper scientific names for his specimens, and that fall the American Museum of Natural History recorded the acquisition of a bat, a dozen mice, a turtle, the skull of a red squirrel and four bird eggs donated by Theodore Roosevelt Jr. The following year, he was learning about taxidermy from John G. Bell, who had prepared specimens for John James Audubon, at his shop on Broadway.

Teedie's specimen gathering increased exponentially at age fourteen. His father sent him next door to consult with Uncle Rob about the best gun to purchase, and the boy was given a French-made 12-gauge shotgun.[90] When he received that first gun, the nearsighted TR wrote in *An Autobiography*, "it puzzled me to find that my companions seemed to see things to shoot at which I could not see at all. One day they read aloud an advertisement in huge letters on a distant billboard, and I then realized that something was the matter, for not only was I unable to read the sign, but I could not even see the letters. I spoke of this to my father, and soon afterwards got my first pair of spectacles, which literally opened an entirely new world to me."[91]

The Roosevelts Leave the Neighborhood

Theodore Sr. and his family lived on East 20th Street until 1873, when the philanthropist decided the neighborhood had changed for the worse and moved uptown to West 57th Street.

"The reason they moved was because the area had become commercialized with the advent of the Ladies Mile with all the big-name stores like Tiffany's, Lord & Taylor and Bergdorf Goodman, on a one-mile stretch of Broadway," Daniel Prebutt told the author. "And as that area became commercialized with these big-name stores. smaller businesses would feed off of the larger entities and not before long, the whole area became commercialized. So the Roosevelts, not liking this, moved uptown to the new posh neighborhood around Central Park. And they could afford it." (See chapter 4.)

After the move, the family rented the 20th Street house until 1896, Prebutt said. Bamie's Uncle James, the family's financial expert, wrote to her when she was living in England to tell her he had sold the brownstone, apparently for $60,000. Photographs of the neighborhood in the early twentieth century show that some of the houses were still standing. But Prebutt said usually at least the two lower floors had been converted into shops, mostly related to the garment industry. Robert B. Roosevelt's house next door, however, was occupied by a café, while another nearby 20th Street building housed a delicatessen.

A *New York Times* article from 1906 noted that the brownstone was sold to the Roosevelt Home Club, an organization of TR's fans who used it for meetings. The *Times*' archives contain another story about the house being sold again in early 1916. "And then, and this is the heartbreaker," Prebutt said, "in the November 16 edition of the *New York Times*, in the real estate section, there's a small paragraph that says, 'Yesterday, the home of former President Roosevelt was demolished,' which means they knocked it down on

The site of Theodore Roosevelt Birthplace at 28 East 20th Street before 1916. *Theodore Roosevelt Collection Photographs: Childhood and Youth, 1858–1880. Theodore Roosevelt Collection, Harvard College Library 560.11-001.*

November 15, 1916. They built another, smaller building in its place, and that only remained for two years."

The curator has heard but cannot confirm that in 1916 when the house was placed on the market, TR's two sisters approached him about whether the house should be purchased to become a museum in his honor and he demurred. "Basically, he said, 'I will not have a shrine made up to me,'" Prebutt related.

While Robert's brownstone next door was also demolished, both houses, or at least replicas of them, returned after the death of Theodore Roosevelt in 1919. That part of the story is told in chapter 6.

4

ROBERT BARNWELL ROOSEVELT

BLACK SHEEP OF THE FAMILY

With his full beard, piercing blue-gray eyes and stern and intelligent countenance, Robert Barnwell Roosevelt resembled his younger brother and next-door neighbor Theodore Sr. But their personalities and interests differed widely.

Robert was born on August 7, 1829, two years before Theodore Sr. While Theodore had no middle name, Robert's was Barnhill, his mother's maiden name. As an adult, leery of what his political opponents might do with a middle name that sounded like a pile of manure, he changed it to Barnwell. His nieces and nephews next door called him Uncle Barnwell.[92]

By all accounts, RBR, as he is known among historians and members of the Roosevelt family, was a brilliant man with an ever-present sense of humor. His grandnephew Nicholas Roosevelt, a conservationist, author and diplomat in his own right, wrote in his 1953 memoir that "Rob loved laughter and to make people laugh" and "had fun in public life."[93] And much like his nephew Theodore, he had a wide range of interests. Because those interests included conservation and crusading against corrupt politicians, a convincing case can be made that TR absorbed those interests from his uncle. As an adult, TR often referred to books written by RBR.

In his wide-ranging career, Robert was a lawyer who practiced from 1850 until 1871, when he was elected to the U.S. House of Representatives, and again in later years after leaving office. His legal success is documented in newspaper clippings he pasted into a scrapbook. Robert was also a crusading newspaper editor, member of the city's Board of Aldermen in 1882, treasurer of the Democratic National Committee in 1892, American minister to the Netherlands from 1888 to 1890 and author of eight books, the majority of them about fish and game birds.[94] The pioneer environmentalist spurred the creation of New York State's fish conservation and management system, which produced hatcheries to reestablish depleted populations.[95] RBR served as president of the Holland Trust Company and was president or director of other financial and insurance companies. An accomplished yachtsman, RBR helped found and lead many clubs. He created and was elected permanent president of the Pot-luck Club, whose eminent literary male and female members cooked their own dinners and wrote songs or parodies about the dishes they contributed. He was a president of the Holland Society and a member of numerous organizations, including the American Association for the Advancement of Science, Chamber of Commerce, Sons of the American Revolution, Municipal Art Society and American Geographical Society.[96] He even wrote a play when he was seventeen that was almost produced commercially, but the financial misfortune of the producer curtailed mounting the show. Even worse, the manuscript was then destroyed in a fire at the Winter Garden Theater.[97]

Robert B. Roosevelt in 1859. *Courtesy Century Association Archives.*

During the Civil War, Robert, like Theodore Sr, did not join the army. But he joined the state militia and actively supported the Union like his brother, helping form various organizations, including the Loyal National League, Union League Club and the Allotment Commission, of which Theodore was also a member. But while Robert and his more distant Hyde Park relatives remained Democrats, Theodore Sr. switched his party affiliation to Republican to support Abraham Lincoln. That decision divided the family into the Oyster Bay Republican and Hyde Park Democratic factions, generating animosity that lingered until late in the twentieth century.[98]

Despite his varied accomplishments, Robert, who enjoyed entertaining avant-garde guests such as Oscar Wilde at his home, was little known after his death. The reasons are that he was overshadowed by his nephew and was considered an embarrassment by his family, which never talked about him. At the time, running for office was considered unseemly in the Roosevelts' elite social circle. But it was Robert's extramarital affairs—particularly having a separate family with a mistress he set up in a household near his own—that so scandalized the Roosevelts for generations. He was commonly referred to as the black sheep in the family tree—if he was discussed at all.

Nicholas Roosevelt was one early exemption, writing in his 1953 memoir:

> *Vigorous, lusty, vital, he was an Elizabethan survival in the Victorian era, an unconventional member of a society and family in which the prudent mores of a provincial mercantile class viewed with disapproval any departure from the accepted norm. Our elders obviously had a serene confidence that the family was—or at least must appear to the world to be—above reproach. The few individuals whose excess of vitality took unconventional forms were ostracized. If ever their names were mentioned in the presence of the youngsters the conversation was quickly turned, and our parents, when pressed, explained that every family has its black sheep, of whom the less said the better.... Uncle Rob cared little for the conventional, and broadcast his thoughts to all who would read or listen to them.*[99]

Unlike Nicholas, other Roosevelts continued to rarely mention Robert to outsiders until the 1980s. Then P. James Roosevelt, RBR's great-grandson and an investment counselor from Oyster Bay, who was the head of the Oyster Bay branch of the family at that point, decided to publicly break the family's silence in a 1985 profile of Robert in *The Newsday Magazine*. "It has been said you may not like a Roosevelt, but you cannot find one that is boring," Roosevelt told a reporter.[100]

A PIONEERING CONSERVATIONIST

There was one interest of Robert's that, while unusual at the time, didn't embarrass his relatives and clearly inspired his nephew. That was his lifelong love of fishing and conservation of wildlife. With RBR, Nicholas Roosevelt wrote, "the restlessness inherited from his father, C.V.S. Roosevelt, took the form of a passion for fishing and hunting."[101] RBR authored a half-dozen books on those subjects. He loved the challenge of fishing, and the five-foot seven-inch, 212-pound (the weight he admitted to) sportsman enjoyed spreading his interest into a group activity where he would delight his guests by telling risqué stories and coming up with gourmet recipes for the catch.

After devoting a great deal of time to researching fish, Robert determined by the middle of the nineteenth century that marine life was being depleted by overfishing, industrial development and pollution as well as the construction of dams that blocked spawning runs.

"His common sense told him that the rapidity with which the country was growing and becoming urbanized would result in the extermination of the country's wildlife," Nicholas Roosevelt said. "His sense of the practical led him to fight for the first measure for conservation in this country."[102]

Robert advocated for both voluntary and legally mandated conservation efforts in his books and articles and through his affiliation with conservation groups. In his 1865 volume *Superior Fishing; or, The Striped Bass, Trout, and Black Bass of the Northern States*, along with offering recipes in a chapter titled "Cookery for Sportsmen," RBR in the middle of the book included a chapter titled "Protection of Fish." In it, he sounded like a forerunner of Rachel Carson in her groundbreaking *Silent Spring* when he wrote that the supply of fish

> *can be exhausted, and its quality easily reduced, is painfully apparent; streams in the neighborhood of New York that formerly were alive with trout are now totally deserted.... The shad that a few years ago swarmed up the Hudson in numbers incomputable have become scarce.... Salmon, most nutritious and noblest of fish, which in ancient days paid their yearly visits in vast numbers...are at present taken nowhere to the southward of Maine, and in but limited quantities even in that wild region.... As the railroad advanced and gave improved facility of travel, so-called sportsmen poured over the country...killing without mercy thousands of trout and hundreds of birds.... The woodcock disappeared from the cold black mud of the springy swamps, trout no longer broke the surface of the noisy rills.... So it has been and will be everywhere, unless the people and the real sportsmen take the matter in hand.... Sportsmen have the greatest stake, for if they would retain for their old age and leave for their children the best preserver of health, a love of field sports, they must protect the game-birds and fish.*

Robert, as usual, offered a remedy. Sportsmen, he argued

> *should discourage, by their conversation and example, all infringement of the law or any cruel or wasteful prosecution of what should be sport.... The first necessity, however, is that proper and uniform enactments should be passed in every portion of our extensive nationality....Laws, however, are not so much to blame as the neglect of their enforcement.... The first duty of sportsmen's clubs and of individual sportsmen, a duty to humanity, to themselves, and to the fellow creatures, is to enforce the game laws....Enforce the law thoroughly, and discontinue unreasonable slaughter, and fish, from their enormous fecundity, must increase immensely. Wanton injury...should be punished...by incarcerating the offender in prison....Mere pecuniary fines are an insufficient punishment....A few months in jail would cure the recklessness....By these means can the seductive little beauties, whether of the feathered, furred, or scaly tribe, that allure us to the great woods, the pleasant meadows, or the sparkling brooks, be preserved through endless time in undiminished abundance...and elevating our moral nature.*[103]

In 1864, RBR joined the New York Sportsmen's Club, composed of about fifty of New York City's more prominent citizens. A decade later, it changed its name to the New York Association for the Protection of Game to better reflect its mission. Robert became vice president and then in 1877 was named president, holding that post until his death in 1906. The association, which became a model for wildlife protection groups around the country, lobbied successfully in Albany for conservation laws while also hiring detectives and filing lawsuits to prosecute violators of fish and game regulations.[104]

Robert B. Roosevelt after 1860. *Library of Congress.*

Nicholas Roosevelt wrote that at the time "it was unthinkable that a man should be restricted in the number of birds or animals he might kill on his own land, or the fish he might catch in his own streams....Only an occasional voice was raised against the wholesale slaughter of game and fowl on public lands in various parts of the country, and only a few ardent fishermen objected to the pollution of streams by the dumping of sawdust, sewage and industrial refuse into them. Rob was one of these, and he objected publicly, frequently and loudly."[105]

An early advocate of "pisciculture," now known as mariculture or fish farming, Robert was president of the American Fish Culturists' Association from 1874 to 1882. He was one of three founders of the New York State Fisheries Commission in 1867 and served, without pay, as a commissioner until 1888, when he was appointed minister to The Hague by President Grover Cleveland. Upon returning to New York, he became commission president in 1879. The commission, which eventually evolved into the New York State Department of Environmental Conservation, successfully bred shad and then whitefish, trout and sturgeon. It established fish hatcheries starting in 1870 in upstate Caledonia followed in the 1880s by others, including one at Cold Spring Harbor on Long Island that survives today as a private nonprofit entity. In 1879, the commission was given the additional task of regulating the shellfish industry and in 1883 responsibility for the game and fish protection force that had been created by the state legislature in 1880.[106]

In 1871, his first year in Congress, RBR successfully introduced legislation to create a U.S. Commission of Fish and Fisheries and later that year to authorize the agency to establish hatcheries on the Atlantic and Pacific coasts to repopulate depleted species.[107] Secretary of State Hamilton Fish, who served from 1869 to 1877, referred a foreign diplomat's question about fishing in America to RBR, calling him "the father of all the fishes."

But fishing was not his only ecological interest. A promoter of organic gardening, he predicted that the last war would be between insects and man, and the insects would win.[108]

A Bohemian Lifestyle

Like Robert, his first wife, Elizabeth Ellis Roosevelt, whom he married in 1850, was unconventional, but in a far different way. Aunt Lizzie Ellis, as she was called by her nieces and nephews next door to distinguish her from another Aunt Lizzie in the family, was described as "unorthodox" by relatives. At the rear of the third floor of their brownstone, she kept a menagerie of guinea pigs, chickens, pigeons, a parrot and even a monkey named Topsy. The monkey, which liked to bite other people, was her favorite pet and she dressed it like a fashionable child in ruffled shirts with gold studs. At one point, Aunt Lizzie went too far, causing a stir in the neighborhood by purchasing a cow that had to be led from East 20th Street to her backyard through the house. It was removed once neighbors threatened to take legal action. On the way back through the house, the cow became so petrified that it had to be blindfolded and dragged with its legs tied.[109]

"I truly believe that Robert had a lot to do with Theodore's interest in animals because Theodore's mother, Mittie, was very particular about the cleanliness of the house," Daniel Prebutt, the National Park Service's museum curator for Manhattan sites, told the author. "So there were no pets in the house. Although later Theodore had his taxidermy prizes, the family never had a pet, which is very unusual for someone like Theodore not to have animals around. But he got that through Robert's house because his wife Elizabeth was eccentric and liked to keep animals."

Lizzie eventually became an invalid who spent most of her time in her bedroom. Robert sought comfort with other women—many other women. It was Robert's shocking lack of morality, as far as the family was concerned, that caused other Roosevelts to try to forget him. Theodore Roosevelt biographer David McCullough, one of the first historians to write about Robert in any depth, described him as being "a bit lax in his morals. He was what polite society referred to as a Bohemian, the kind of man who kept company with 'actresses and such.'" In sharp contrast to his maritally faithful and morally strict younger brother and nephew Theodore, RBR was known to have affairs with many women in Manhattan. A story handed down through the family is that he would purchase gaudy green gloves in bulk on sale at A.T. Stewart's department store and give pairs to his conquests so that people who knew him would be on the lookout for the gloves as their wearers strolled on Fifth Avenue or drove through the parks.[110]

But Robert's most scandalous behavior—one that caused a permanent break with his brother next door and other family members—was his relationship with mistress Marion O'Shea. The late Richard Harmond, a retired history professor at St. John's University on Long Island who spent many years researching RBR, surmised the couple met when O'Shea, better known as Minnie, was hired by the *New York Citizen*. It was a political newspaper edited and partly owned by Roosevelt that published from 1864 until 1873. He not only had an affair with Minnie but also set her up in a house on East 20th Street near his home and proceeded to have a secret second family with her. By 1869, she was already pregnant with their first child. The cover story was that Minnie was the widow of a soldier from Scotland, Robert F. Fortescue. It was only years later that his double life was uncovered thanks to genealogical research done by descendants of Robert and Minnie.[111]

The personal schism between Robert and Theodore Sr. was reinforced by a physical separation in 1873 when the younger brother moved the family uptown to 57th Street alongside sibling James Alfred. Robert did not join them at the new location.

A year after Lizzie's death in 1887 after thirty-seven years of marriage, Robert married Minnie in a Catholic church in the London suburb of Clapham in England with no other members of his family present. By that point, his two sons and daughter with Lizzie were grown. They were Margaret Barnhill Roosevelt (1851–1927); John Ellis Roosevelt (1853–1939), a lawyer with his father's Wall Street firm of Roosevelt & Kobbe; and Robert Barnhill Roosevelt Jr. (1866–1929). RBR Jr.'s primary residence was in Washington, D.C., and his career was managing his family's Sayville estate on Long Island, worth $3 million at the time of his death, according to his *New York Times* obituary.

RBR adopted his "Fortescue" offspring: Kenyon Fortescue (1871–1939), Granville Roland "Rolly" Fortescue (1875–1952) and Maude Fortescue (1880–1961).[112] Kenyon also became an attorney with Roosevelt & Kobbe. Granville was a corporal in his first cousin Theodore's Rough Riders in the Spanish-American War and injured his foot in the famous charge up San Juan Hill. He served as a first lieutenant in the 26th Volunteer Infantry during the 1899–1901 insurrection in the Philippines. He was then a second lieutenant in the regular army's 4th Cavalry. After graduating from the Army General Service and Staff College in 1904, he became a first lieutenant in the Tenth United States Cavalry and was appointed by President Theodore Roosevelt as a White House military aide. He resigned from the army in 1906 and then served as a captain with the Cuban Rural Guard until resigning three years later to become a war correspondent in Morocco for the *London Standard*. He reported in Europe during World War I for the *London Daily Telegraph*. When the United States entered the war in 1917, he served as a major in the 314th Field Artillery with the American Expeditionary Force in France and was gassed during a German attack. Granville remained in the army until 1928, retiring with the rank of major.

After marrying Grace Hubbard Bell, niece of the inventor Alexander Graham Bell, in 1910, he had a messy personal life marked by a refusal to engage in any form of steady employment after leaving the military. He is buried at Arlington National Cemetery, the only Roosevelt interred there. Maude married an English lawyer and moved to London. Minnie died in Atlantic City in 1902.[113]

Despite their overlapping interests, TR kept his distance from his uncle until more than five years after the death of Theodore Sr., probably to respect his father's wishes. But starting around 1900, there was an increasing flow of letters between uncle and nephew, and RBR was even invited to TR's inauguration in 1905. Afterward, the president wrote to his uncle from the White House, saying, "Dear Uncle Rob, it was particularly pleasant having you here."

Despite their shared interests in conservation, politics and public service and despite their proximity during Theodore's childhood, TR only mentions his uncle once in his 1920 book *Theodore Roosevelt: An Autobiography*. And that reference has nothing to do with whatever influence Robert had on his nephew. It concerns his Aunt Anna: "She knew all the 'Br'er Rabbit' stories, and I was brought up on them. One of my uncles, Robert Roosevelt, was much struck with them, and took them down from her dictation, publishing them in *Harper's*, where they fell flat. This was a good many years before a genius arose who in 'Uncle Remus' made the stories immortal."[114]

Robert's descendants have increasingly embraced his legacy in recent decades. They noted that divorce was impossible for a person of Robert's stature, no matter how peculiar his first wife acted. "His lifestyle would not be considered extreme by today's standards," great-grandson P. James Roosevelt remarked in 1985.[115]

Tweed Roosevelt of Boston, a great-grandson of TR and former head of the Theodore Roosevelt Association, said in a February 23, 2021 podcast that "RBR was both a saint and a sinner. As a young man in his twenties he was quite the ladies' man. His taste ran to showgirls and dancers, and they were no doubt bowled over by his status and money....Eventually, he settled down and got married. And this is when he started his good works. He was a very early conservationist and ecologist, before the term was even invented....TR idolized him and he became a role model for TR's later success in this area."

A LIFELONG INTEREST IN GOVERNMENT AND POLITICS

Along with conservation, involvement in politics remained a constant in RBR's life. William Marcy "Boss" Tweed was already running the Tammany Hall Democratic machine in New York City when RBR upset his Republican Oyster Bay branch of the family relatives by deciding to run, successfully, for Congress as a Democrat in 1870. In the House of Representatives, he spoke out about a political ring that was controlling the District of Columbia. His efforts were recognized by the citizens of the capital, who presented him with a gold-headed cane. RBR lasted only one term, from 1871 to 1873, before deciding he wasn't suited for life in Washington.

Even though he had been elected with the help of Tammany Hall, Robert became a determined enemy of Tweed. When the boss's corruption was revealed, RBR and other reform Democrats held a public meeting at Cooper Union, where Roosevelt was one of the speakers who captivated the audience. Anyone caught tampering with a ballot box should be shot on sight, the reformer bellowed. He accused the Tweed ring of undermining liberty. Although he played only a supporting role in Tweed's downfall, he did help organize The Committee of Seventy, a citizens' reform group that helped force Tweed out of his position in 1871.[116]

RBR was a leading advocate for the creation of a paid city fire department and for replacing an out-of-date and inefficient Sanitary Board with a paid city health department.

As TR's trajectory in government rose, his uncle mostly bowed out of politics to avoid embarrassing him. For that reason, in 1904 he refused his party's designation as a presidential elector, although he was a delegate at other national Democratic Party conventions.[117]

Robert was back in the news again as a new reform trustee of the Brooklyn Bridge project in its eleventh year of construction, serving from 1879 to 1881. He also generated headlines—negative ones—when he called on the city government to create municipal construction jobs to prevent an uprising by the poor. "Let us try some plan and convince the poor that we have the blood of civilized men in our veins," he wrote. The newspapers denounced him as a fool.[118]

Embracing the Country Life

When he wasn't crusading about stamping out government corruption or saving wildlife, RBR would allow his dry sense of humor to emerge. This was evidenced in his 1871 satirical volume about the differences between men and women, *Progressive Petticoats; Or, Dressed to Death. The Autobiography of a Married Man*, and in his 1869 book titled *Five Acres Too Much.*

In *Progressive Petticoats,* Robert wrote that the book is "purely jocose and ironical, intended only as a harmless pleasantry" and "nothing could be further from my intentions than to cast a slur on the sex" and "that I am entirely satisfied, firmly convinced, and altogether persuaded, that I have the best wife in the world." Then he opines, "There is one peculiarity about the female character which seems to be universal with the sex; they are unable to appreciate a joke, especially where that joke bears a little against themselves." He goes on to say, "Women as a class have a mission. Our households are their natural happy hunting-grounds. The health and happiness of the human race are in their keeping."

In *Five Acres Too Much*, RBR pokes fun at the then-fashionable practice among the gentry of heading to the country to establish self-sufficient farms. He wrote that he authored the book in response to "a little volume called *Ten Acres Enough*" in which a "charming and interesting account is given of the successful attempt of a Philadelphia mechanic to redeem a strip of exhausted land of ten acres. So useful is the instruction it contains, that no one should think of buying a farm, experimenting in rural life, or even reading this book, without first perusing that one. To be sure the author forgets occasionally some minor matters—such as clothing, food, and the like, leaving his family naked and unfed for several years."

Then RBR goes on to lay out the virtues of country living in flowery marathon run-on sentences:

> *The country—how beautiful it is! To a man wearied with the cares of city life; who has pursued an exhausting profession for several years with vigorous energy; who has taken a hand in politics, attended caucuses and Conventions, and helped to "run the machine"; who has a philanthropic turn of mind, and gone on committees and made public collections; and who, moreover, has abundant means—this, the last, is by no means least—the country, with its green leaves, its lovely flowers, its waving grass, its early vegetables, and its luscious fruits, is most attractive; and where a residence can be obtained which combines all these luxuries with*

pure air, and no chills and fever, and which is not too remote from city life and its attractions, it is as near to Paradise as this world permits.[119]

Robert discounts most areas around the city as a potential paradise, showing particular disdain for Staten Island, which he wrote "is overrun by sour-krout-eating, lager-beer-drinking" Germans. His "Eden of a country village" is Flushing on the northern edge of Queens County on Long Island, where he owned "the five acres that this book is all about." RBR decided to build a country house and develop a farm there.[120]

Robert devoted chapters to each of the projects in creating the farm, such as buying a cow. "A cow is model…for a wife," he wrote. "She is gentle, good, and beautiful and makes a fuss." After his first year as a gentleman farmer, RBR wrote that he had "shown how readily a person can pass from the profession of a lawyer to that of an agriculturalist." He noted that "the weather has been exceptionally hot and dry" and "my furniture was badly damaged in being transported from the city to the country" so that "the profit, therefore, must be looked for, not in the merely vulgar, material sense, but somewhat in the sensations, thoughts, and experiences that were included in the results of the year's labor." He said his cost for building the house and establishing the farm was almost $16,000, but he calculated that he saved $2,000 by not traveling to Newport or Saratoga for the summer. As a result, "the profits of my first year were not large, but sufficient to induce me to continue the experiment."[121]

"Our second year," he wrote later in the book, "was certainly a great advance upon the first, as the former might be said to have been rather a case for what the merchants call profit and loss—all loss and no profit, so far as actual production is concerned. The previous attempt had resulted in raising absolutely nothing, whereas our subsequent one had raised a great deal; we had much to show for it, although not always what we wanted." He said his expenses for the second year were $76.50 and his proceeds $277.50. "Taking all these things into consideration, I resolved to abandon the city… to devote myself to agricultural pursuits." RBR, however, never abandoned Manhattan but did continue to spend time in the country.[122]

In 1873, the year he left Congress, Robert purchased 215 acres on a lake in Sayville on the south shore of Long Island in Suffolk County. Besides his 5 acres in Flushing, he also owned land in New Jersey and Texas. On the Sayville property, he built a large wooden frame house he called Lotus Lake. Later, his two sons with Lizzie, Robert Jr. and John, built adjoining houses. He loved fishing, hunting and sailing on the Great South Bay. And he enjoyed the distance from his disapproving relatives up in Oyster Bay. Robert also moved his secret Fortescue family to Sayville.[123]

Robert, Robert Jr. and John became infamous locally for racing buckboards pulled by teams of charging horses along dusty local roads from the train station to their property. The situation escalated in 1904, the *New York World* reported on May 17 under a headline reading "Uncle of the President and His Two Sons Burn Up the Long Island Roads." Father and sons had purchased speedy imported automobiles, among the first on Long Island, and then raced them to their property as local townspeople lined up to witness the irresistible event. The reporter said RBR, who was often referred to as Uncle Rob or Uncle Barnwell in written accounts of the time, was wearing "the most approved automobile clothing" and was driving himself with his long gray hair curling from beneath his helmet. RBR "acts as his own chauffeur, something his distinguished nephew has not yet had the hardihood to attempt." Robert finished first.[124]

Later Years

As much as he enjoyed his summers in Sayville and farming in Flushing, evidence that Robert never fully abandoned the city, or politics, was his election to the Board of Aldermen in 1882. In 1888, he was appointed by President Grover Cleveland as the minister to The Hague, where he served for two years. He was named treasurer of the Democratic National Committee in 1892.[125]

RBR also never gave up on public causes and public discourse. His last notoriety arose from suggesting a change in the layout of Central Park, including removing the stone wall along 5th Avenue to widen the roadway. As usual, his suggestion caused an uproar.

The stout Robert, who suffered with gout from his mid-twenties on and drank lemon juice in an attempt to cure it, died at Lotos Lake at age seventy-six on June 14, 1906. He

Robert B. Roosevelt depicted in *Frank Leslie's Illustrated Newspaper* on May 26, 1888, after his appointment as United States minister to the Netherlands. *Author photo.*

was buried in the family plot at Green-Wood Cemetery in Brooklyn. His Sayville house remained vacant and was vandalized until it was destroyed in an arson fire in 1958. His son John Ellis's house and estate, Meadow Croft, is now owned by Suffolk County.

Nicholas Roosevelt, who had met Robert only once, at TR's inauguration in 1905 when he was eleven and RBR was almost eighty, wrote that "Uncle Rob was a salty old bird...and got more fun out of life than many of those whose silence about him failed to hide a prim distaste for the manner in which he insisted on living his own life in his own way, instead of theirs."[126]

5

THEODORE SR. MOVES THE FAMILY UPTOWN

Robert B. Roosevelt and his brother Theodore—already separated by their disparate personalities, politics and morals—became physically separated in 1873 when the younger sibling moved his family uptown next to his brother James Alfred and left RBR behind. With his large inheritance from his father, Cornelius Van Schaack Roosevelt, Theodore easily had the means to build a new impressive house uptown as well as enjoy other luxuries.

As noted in chapter 3, Theodore decided to move farther north in Manhattan along with many others of his social class when the area south of Union Square along Broadway began to become commercialized by large department stores. One of them, Lord & Taylor, was moving to a new building at Broadway and 20th Street, less than a block from Theodore's home. Smaller shops, mostly related to the garment trade, were spreading onto the adjacent cross streets. The grand old home of Theodore's father on Union Square already had been demolished and replaced by a sewing-machine factory.[127]

To escape the changing neighborhood downtown, Theodore and James Alfred purchased adjoining lots on the south side of 57th Street just west of 5th Avenue. They were two blocks from fashionable Central Park, which had opened in 1858. The brothers both hired architect Russell Sturgis, a designer of Gothic country estates that were wildly popular, to design their homes. The new structures would be far less modest than the brownstone on East 20th Street, with woodwork and furniture custom-made in Philadelphia using designs by another popular architect, Frank Furness.[128]

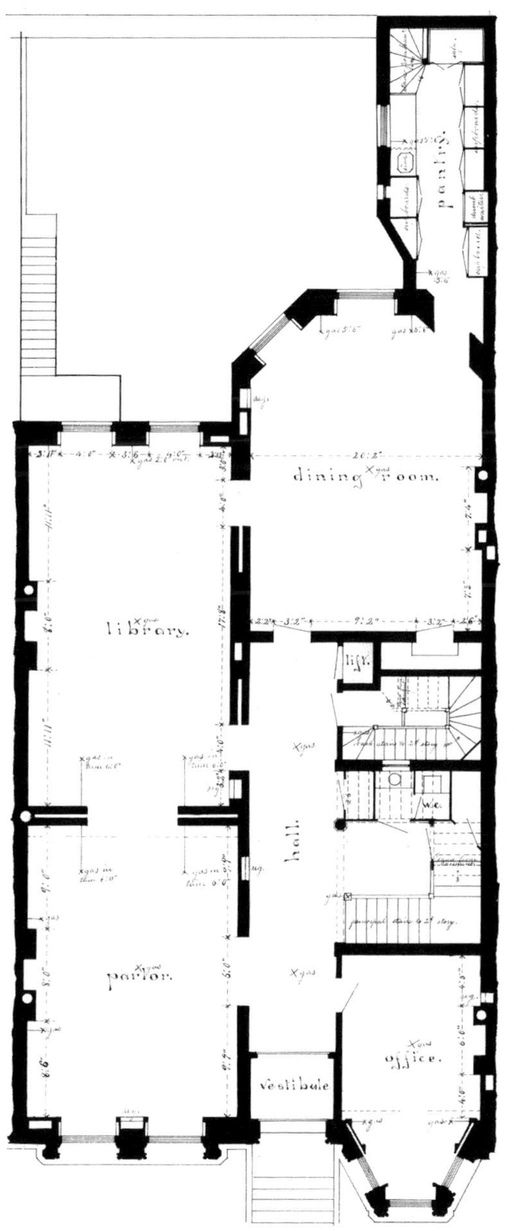

First-floor plan of 6 West 57th Street. *Courtesy of Sagamore Hill National Historic Site, National Park Service, Oyster Bay, NY.*

Since Theodore believed firmly that the best education was travel, he took the family on an extended trip to Egypt, the Holy Land and southeastern and central Europe to avoid the initial chaos of construction. Then the children were left with a German family in Dresden for five months to learn the language and culture while Mittie and older daughter Bamie traveled to Paris and the spa resort town of Carlsbad in what is now the Czech Republic.

Theodore returned alone in the summer of 1873 to oversee the final construction of their new home. While staying at the Union League Club, Theodore pursued a hectic life that kept him in a "perpetual rush" from six o'clock in the morning until often almost midnight. He began each day by checking on the house before heading off to work at Roosevelt & Son, where orders for plate glass had expanded exponentially after the Great Chicago Fire in October 1871. Meanwhile, his philanthropic enterprises were taking up more and more time of his time. But as Theodore reiterated in a letter to Bamie in September, he always preferred activity to inactivity, noting that "you know I never approved of rusting out."[129]

Exterior view of 4–8 West 57th Street by Albert Levy taken between 1883 and 1895. The Roosevelts lived at No. 6. *The Art Institute of Chicago*.

The furniture from East 20th Street was moved uptown and augmented by new purchases. Theodore in New York and Mittie in Paris corresponded about family matters and arrangements for the new house. She told her husband she was buying china soap dishes and bolts of claret-colored cloth for new livery for the servants. He was hiring more of "the family downstairs" because a bigger staff would be needed to manage the larger home. He said a marble mantelpiece had arrived and a new furnace had been installed. The carpet she had picked out in Paris had been delivered. He had ordered gas fixtures and noted that the old chandelier from the 20th Street library seemed to look right in his new study. "I have left the billiard room without any chandelier at present, only sidelights, so if you do find it will answer for dancing it will not be in your way," he wrote. Unfortunately, the items ordered from Philadelphia—furniture, woodwork and a huge hand-carved front staircase—were behind schedule. When the staircase did arrive and was installed, it failed to connect with the second floor. The three-foot gap resulted from the architect giving the wrong measurements to the manufacturer. The staircase had to be removed and remade.[130]

Despite the setbacks, Theodore was extremely pleased, declaring that there was no better-built house in the city. But he was not happy with every detail. He noticed the architect had used imitation oak beams made of plaster in the front hall ceiling. He wrote to his wife that he had ordered them replaced with real wood even if it "seems hard to destroy so much beautifully finished work." But he knew Mittie would not be happy with anything artificial in her new home.[131] He wrote to Bamie that "I can see all who pass in Fifth Avenue nicely from your room." He added that he had "just came in time to save a bathtub from going, as originally intended, into your closet."[132]

With construction continuing, Theodore moved in on October 5. There still was no front staircase, and other work was going on when the rest of the family arrived on the *Russia* exactly one month later, as was reported in the *New York Times* on November 6. The expanded staff—Dora Watkins, Mary Ann, a footman named Frank and four or five other additions, including a Sophie, Mary, George and a Black groom named Davis—moved everything from downtown into 6 West 57th Street from a line of vehicles that stretched all the way down the block.[133]

While Theodore Sr.'s letters contain many irritated references to the electric call system to his stables and the speaking tubes from his family's rooms to beckon the servants not working and the gas lights being installed incorrectly, the completed house could not fail to impress.[134]

The entrance hall at 6 West 57th Street. *Theodore Roosevelt Collection Photographs: Childhood and Youth, 1858–1880. Theodore Roosevelt Collection, Harvard College Library 560.11-016.*

Theodore Roosevelt biographer David McCullough wrote that

> *the house was a showplace, even by the extravagant standards being set in the vicinity along upper Fifth Avenue. There was no resemblance whatever to the house on East 20th Street.... Rooms, hallways, mirrors, fireplaces, bookcases, furniture, everything was larger and infinitely more luxurious. There were tremendous mirrors everywhere, tasseled chandeliers, walls of glassed-in books, intricately carved sliding doors, paneled and tiled fireplaces, huge curtains, inlaid woods, polished silver, Persian rugs. East 20th Street had had a degree of restraint, even simplicity—or at least simplicity as understood by mid-Victorians. There the furniture had been largely the standard pieces for the standard domestic gentility....But the sumptuous pieces conceived by Furness are all one-of-a-kind, all of rich inlaid woods and mighty in scale—great hand-carved, leather-upholstered, brass-studded dining room chairs, heavy as thrones and broad enough to accommodate even the very largest of that era's well-fed gentry; a bed for the master of the house and his lady that might have been commissioned for an Oriental potentate. Windows were few and heavily curtained, closing off the world beyond.*[135]

Top: Library at 6 West 57th Street. *Theodore Roosevelt Collection Photographs: Childhood and Youth, 1858–1880. Theodore Roosevelt Collection, Harvard College Library 560.11-017.*

Bottom: Another view of the library at 6 West 57th Street. *Theodore Roosevelt Collection Photographs: Childhood and Youth, 1858–1880. Theodore Roosevelt Collection, Harvard College Library 560.11-018.*

The dining room at 6 West 57th Street. *Theodore Roosevelt Collection Photographs: Childhood and Youth, 1858–1880. Theodore Roosevelt Collection, Harvard College Library 560.11-019.*

A fully equipped gymnasium was situated on the top floor with space for Teedie's museum in the attic.

There are few surviving records of Theodore's spending on the house. Bamie years later remarked in unpublished reminiscences that her mother's European buying spree to furnish the house "proved rather fatal to the family fortunes."[136] But there is no documentation to show that, and Theodore continued to spend lavishly after the house was completed. The construction delays did have one documented effect on Bamie. Her debut into society, which was to have taken place in the house before Christmas, was not held until January. In the meantime, her father arranged for a dance in her honor in Philadelphia. The house was so large that when the family finally staged Bamie's "at home" debut, Mittie sent out about five hundred invitations. But there seemed to be little gossip about the ostentation because of Theodore's solid reputation for good works.[137]

Once settled in, Mittie organized a dancing class in the house for her three youngest children and others from their circle, about forty in total.[138]

Theodore Sr., meanwhile, characteristically put the house to charitable use. Corinne Roosevelt Robinson later wrote that her father founded the city's orthopedic hospital because her older sister Bamie

> *suffered from spinal trouble, and my father was determined to leave no stone unturned to make her body fit for life's joys and life's labors. He could not at first influence sufficient people to start the building of a hospital, and he decided that if the New York public could only see what the new instruments would do for the stricken children, that it could be aroused to assist the enterprise. And so, one beautiful spring afternoon, my mother gave what was supposed to be a purely social reception at our second home, at 6 W. 57th Street, and my father saw to it that the little sufferers in whom he was interested were brought from their poverty-stricken homes to ours and laid upon our dining room table, with the steel appliances which could help them back to normal limbs on their backs and legs, thus ready to visualize to New York citizens how the stricken little people might be cured. He placed me by the table where the children lay, and explained to me how I could show the appliances, and what they were supposed to achieve; and I can still hear the voice of the first Mrs. John Jacob Astor, as she leaned over one fragile-looking child and, turning to my father, said: "Theodore, you are right; these children must be restored and made into active citizens again, and I for one will help you in your work." That very day enough money was donated to start the first Orthopaedic Hospital, in East 59th Street.*[139]

Theodore Roosevelt as Harvard freshman in December 1876. *Theodore Roosevelt Collection Photographs: Childhood and Youth, 1858–1880. Theodore Roosevelt Collection, Harvard College Library 520.12-001.*

"The winter of 1874 was passed at our new home," Corinne wrote. "My brother was still considered too delicate to send to a boarding-school, and various tutors were engaged for his education, which my brother Elliott and I shared."[140] The primary task of the tutors was to prepare Theodore Jr. for the Harvard College entrance examination. He was admitted in 1876.

Young Theodore continued his favorite pursuits on West 57th Street. He worked out on the parallel bars, boxed and wrestled in the gymnasium. Tutor Arthur Cutler noted that his young charge spent an equal amount of time on his studies and physical activity. The asthma attacks were occurring less frequently. With a room on the top floor serving as a natural history museum, Theodore continued shooting, skinning and stuffing specimens. In one letter to Bamie he wrote that he was writing in a "rather smelly room as the fresh skins of six night herons are reposing on the table beside me."[141]

Theodore Roosevelt in September 1875. *Theodore Roosevelt Collection Photographs: Childhood and Youth, 1858–1880. Theodore Roosevelt Collection, Harvard College Library 520.11-008.*

When Elliott began to suffer from severe headaches and dizzy spells, his father sent him abroad in 1874 and to the South in 1875 to stay with a friend who was a doctor, hoping that two months in the outdoors hunting would build up his constitution. This was followed by two visits to an army fort in Texas totaling more than a year in 1876–77.[142]

With its glass importing business battered by an economic depression and also suffering from increasing domestic manufacturing competition, the family sold its operation to a British firm in 1876. With Roosevelt & Son now engaged solely in private banking and investment, Theodore no longer commuted to Maiden Lane but to new offices on Pine Street.[143]

Elliott returned home in 1877 with his health improved only to see his father decline. After Theodore Jr. had returned to Harvard for his sophomore year that fall, his father experienced intestinal distress. He was suffering from acute peritonitis or severe inflammation of the bowels, according to the doctors' initial diagnosis. But it was later determined that he was dying from an inoperable fibrous tumor of the bowel. Elliott barely left Theodore Sr.'s room as his father suffered from agonizing pain only partially relieved by chloroform as his hair turned gray. "He was so mad with pain that beyond groans and horrible writhes and twists he could do nothing," Elliott wrote in a private recollection. "Oh my God my father what agonies you suffered."[144]

On Saturday, February 9, 1878, Theodore at Harvard received a telegram from the family telling him to come home at once. "The best physicians searched in vain for a remedy for the hidden trouble," Corinne wrote, "and the gay young college sophomore was recalled to a house of mourning."[145] Theodore Sr. died that day at age forty-six. Elliott described the scene in a letter written the following day. With newsboys and orphans helped by his father huddling on the steps of 6 West 57th Street, Elliott said he heard "the gurgling breathing of death.…His eyelids fluttered, he gave three breaths." His mother cried out: "I expect he is safe in the arms of Jesus now!"[146]

Corinne wrote,

> *In spite of the sorrow, in spite of a sense of the irreparable loss, there was something infinitely inspiring in the days preceding and following my father's death. When New York City knew that its benefactor lay in extreme illness, it seemed as if the whole city came to the door of his house to ask news of him. How well I remember the day before his death, when the papers had announced that there was but little hope of his recovery. The crowd of individuals who filled 57th Street in their effort to hear the physicians' bulletin concerning his condition was huge and varied. Newsboys from the West Side Lodging House, little Italian girls from his Sunday-school class, sat for hours on the stone steps of 6 West 57th Street, our second home, waiting with anxious intensity for news of the man who meant more to them than any other human being had ever meant before; and those more fortunate ones who had known him in another way drove unceasingly up in their carriages to the door and looked with sympathetic interest at the children of the slums who shared with them such a sense of bitter bereavement and loss in the premature death of one so closely connected with all sides of his beloved native city.*[147]

Theodore Roosevelt circa 1877. *Theodore Roosevelt Collection Photographs: Childhood and Youth, 1858–1880. Theodore Roosevelt Collection, Harvard College Library 520.11-011.*

Now the only Theodore Roosevelt, the elder son, grieved that he had not done more for his father while he was ill and had not been able to see him before he died. In his diary, he made a slash of black ink down the page for February 9 and wrote, "My dear Father. Born Sept. 23, 1831." The following two days, he wrote nothing. He began his entry on February 12 by saying, "He has just been buried. I shall never forget these terrible three days."[148]

While Mittie had always been eccentric, her quirks became more pronounced after the death of her husband. The ever-dutiful Bamie took over more responsibility for the family from her mother, whom she began to view with scorn. In Corinne's debutante season, her mother would wait up for her when she came back from a dance. Concerned that intruders might enter the house, Mittie made her daughter recite a password phrase—"How does the busy bee improve each shining hour"—before she would be admitted.[149]

Theodore returned to Harvard for his junior year in the fall of 1878. On October 18, 1878, he met the girl of his dreams, "rare and radiant maiden" Alice Lee, on a weekend visit to the home of a classmate. Richard Saltonstall's family lived next door to the Lees at Chestnut Hill, six miles from campus. TR immediately knew that he wanted to marry the vivacious, intelligent and beautiful seventeen-year-old girl, two years younger than him. When she initially rebuffed his proposals, Theodore persisted, and by January 1880, Alice had consented to marry him. Her father wanted a long engagement, thinking she was still too young to be a bride. Mittie, who hosted dozens of teas, dinners and other events at 57th Street to show off Alice, resolved that logjam by proposing that the couple live with her. The wedding was held at the Unitarian church in Brookline, Massachusetts, on October 27, 1880, TR's twenty-second birthday. Elliott was the best man. The only non-Roosevelt invited by the groom was family friend Edith Carow, whom many who knew them had assumed was the woman Theodore would marry.

The newlyweds postponed a planned trip to Europe because Theodore had decided to enroll in law school at the urging of his attorney-uncle Robert. Instead, the couple honeymooned briefly at Tranquility, the home Theodore Sr. had rented for summers in Oyster Bay, before returning to live with Mittie on West 57th Street on Saturday, November 13. They lived in an apartment on the third floor, and TR presided as the head of the family.[150]

On April 29, 1882, Corinne married Scottish-born Douglas Robinson (1855–1918), a wealthy older financier and real estate broker who was a great-nephew of President James Monroe and a friend of her brother Elliott.

The wedding followed a six-month engagement that she kept thinking about breaking off because he did not measure up to her father and brothers.[151]

That winter, Theodore pursued his literary interests by working on his first major book, *The Naval War of 1812*, the first of thirty-eight he would write. He became involved in many of the organizations supported by his father before deciding that charity work had little interest for him. He studied at Columbia Law School, then located in an old house downtown on Great Jones Street. Theodore left the house at 7:30 a.m. and walked the fifty-four blocks down 5th Avenue every morning in time for an 8:30 a.m. class. Some afternoons he read cases in his uncle's law office. Then he walked the roughly three miles home, saying it was the only exercise he could work into his busy life. "The law work is very interesting," Theodore wrote in his diary. "I like the law school work very much." But soon he would decide that a legal career was not for him and shifted his focus to politics and public service.[152] That summer, the couple traveled to Europe for a belated honeymoon.

Back in New York, Theodore and Alice kept a busy social schedule because the Roosevelts were an old-money proper society family and as such were acknowledged to be part of the "400" recognized by Caroline Astor, the arbiter of such matters. They attended dinners with the Astors and other prominent families and spent Monday nights at the opera. "Every moment of my time occupied," TR wrote in his diary.[153]

As Theodore's interest in a political career grew, he spent more time with political bosses and others who could guide him in that direction. The political leader with whom TR spent the most time was Joseph Murray, who became a mentor and helped persuade young Roosevelt to become part of the "governing class." He was nominated as the Republican candidate for a Manhattan state assembly seat in the Twenty-First "Silk Stocking" District. He won in November and on January 1, 1882, became an elected public servant. At age twenty-three, he was the youngest member ever to serve in that chamber. "The Young Reformer," as he was quickly dubbed, spent part of the week in Albany and generally returned to Manhattan on Fridays.[154]

Theodore had been thinking since the honeymoon in Oyster Bay about building a permanent home for his new family in that area. Because his father had given away so much money, TR could afford only one home; he could not maintain both a city house and a summer house in the country like others in his social class. In the fall after the honeymoon, Theodore purchased 155 acres on Cove Neck near Oyster Bay and then sold parcels to Bamie and his Aunt Anna to reduce his outlay. He had a stable built on the ninety-five acres he had kept for himself in the fall of 1883 as the

Corinne Roosevelt. *National Park Service—Theodore Roosevelt Birthplace NHS.*

first step in creating a homestead. But he had no immediate plans to build a house—to be known as Leeholm, or "home for his wife," Alice Lee, in Dutch—because his focus was on the assembly.[155]

Theodore and Alice eventually moved into a house of their own on West 45th Street. Historians disagree on whether they owned or rented the brownstone. It was next to the home of Corinne and Douglas Robinson, who in April 1882 had become the parents of Theodore Douglas Robinson, the first child of the next generation. The arrangement allowed Alice to remain in the city while TR was in Albany. "I can imagine nothing more happy in life than an evening spent in my cozy little sitting room, before a bright fire of soft coal, my books all around me, and playing backgammon with my own dainty mistress," Theodore wrote in his diary that winter.[156]

In early 1884, Alice was pregnant and due to give birth in mid-February, while TR was busy with politics and spending little time with his wife. So Theodore had her move from their brownstone into their old apartment on the third floor of the family home at 6 West 57th Street so his mother and sisters could look after Alice while he was in Albany. The Roosevelt women doted on Alice, but she craved the company of her husband. When he arrived for the weekend, his wife would be waiting at the door. Corinne told Alice that she could "share him" with his mother and sisters. Corinne and her husband lived on the third floor with Alice so it could serve as a nursery for their son and Alice's baby when it arrived.[157]

Anna "Bamie" Roosevelt. *Courtesy of Sagamore Hill National Historic Site, National Park Service, Oyster Bay, NY.*

On February 12, Alice went into labor after TR had left for Albany that morning. Their daughter, Alice, was born that night. Roosevelt received a telegram the next morning at the capitol saying that the new mother was "only fairly well," not unexpected after delivering a first child, and their daughter was healthy. A few hours later, a second telegraph arrived, urging him to return to the city immediately. The exact wording has not been recorded. Theodore rushed for the next train to make the 145-mile journey south.[158]

Mittie Roosevelt in later years. *Courtesy of Sagamore Hill National Historic Site, National Park Service, Oyster Bay, NY.*

The trip would normally take about five hours. But because of heavy fog, the train did not reach Grand Central Station until 10:30 p.m. It was so foggy that TR had to navigate from streetlight to streetlight and noted that it "looked as though gray curtains had been drawn around them." He did not reach 6 West 57th Street until almost midnight. The only light was burning in a third-story window. When Theodore rang the bell, most historical accounts state that Elliott flung open the door and proclaimed, "There is a curse on this house. Mother is dying and Alice is dying too." David McCullough, however, contended those words were spoken by Elliott to Corinne and her husband when they arrived around 10:30 p.m.[159]

Mittie, who had been fanatical about the cleanliness of her home, had contracted typhoid fever from contaminated water or food. Alice was suffering with Bright's disease, a kidney ailment not diagnosed during her pregnancy. But daughter Alice was doing well. TR rushed to his wife's bedside, where she barely recognized him. He had held her for two hours when he was told that if he wished to see his mother alive again, he needed to come down to her room. TR was standing at her bedside with his three siblings when she died at three o'clock in the morning, and he repeated the words Elliott had used: "There is a curse on this house." He climbed back to the third floor and took Alice in his arms again. She held on until two o'clock that afternoon. Alice, only twenty-two, had also died on Valentine's Day—the fourth anniversary of their engagement.[160] In his diary page for that day, Theodore drew a large X and wrote, "The light has gone out of my life."[161]

The newspapers took note of the extraordinary loss in such a prominent family. "Seldom, if ever, has New York society received such a shock as yesterday in [these] sad and sudden deaths," the *New York World* wrote on

February 15, 1884. The *New York Tribune* commented that "the loss of his wife and mother in a single day is a terrible affliction."

Corinne wrote that "the great tragedy of his young wife's death at the birth of her first child was an even greater tragedy because the death of our lovely mother occurred [less than] twenty-four hours before her son's wife passed away. Our mother's home at 57th Street had been the background of our young married life, as it had been the foreground of our youth, and the winter of 1884 had been spent by my husband and myself at 6 West 57th Street, and the consequence was that as Theodore also made his headquarters there, we had been much together, and that very fact made it even harder to break up the home which had been so long the centre of our family life."[162]

The double funeral was held at the Fifth Avenue Presbyterian Church on February 16. Theodore and his three siblings were joined by Alice's father in the front pew. Before them rested two rosewood coffins covered with roses and lilies of the valley while two hearses waited outside. The large church was filled with the city's social and political elite.[163]

The day after Mittie and Alice were buried at Green-Wood Cemetery in Brooklyn alongside Theodore Sr. and Grandma Bulloch, TR had his daughter, wearing a locket containing her mother's hair, christened Alice Lee. Then her father turned her over to unmarried thirty-year-old Bamie, which was the only positive development for her during the miserable weekend.[164]

Soon after, the siblings decided to sell 6 West 57th Street, which had become increasingly expensive to maintain as the family's fortune was eroded by Mittie's lavish entertaining of the city's elite. It was purchased in less than a week by John S. Kennedy. He was a wealthy longtime friend of Theodore Sr. and a fellow director of the American Museum of Natural History whose banking firm was J.S. Kennedy & Company. The sale agreement stipulated that the Roosevelts would have to vacate the house by the end of April. It was left to Bamie to handle the details, as usual.

6
THE LATER HOMES OF THE OYSTER BAY ROOSEVELTS

By the time Mittie's four children decided to sell the house at 6 West 57th Street soon after her death on Valentine's Day in 1884, Corinne and Elliott were already married with their own homes. Bamie would soon buy one. And Theodore would build his residence at Sagamore Hill in Oyster Bay that year.

As mentioned in the previous chapter, Corinne had married Douglas Robinson on April 29, 1882. The couple lived on West 45th Street except when they stayed at the West 57th Street house during the pregnancy of Theodore's wife, Alice.

Elliott

After Theodore graduated from Harvard in 1880, he and his younger brother spent two months hunting out west, and then Elliott headed to India for another hunting trip. When he returned home, Elliott lived in the West 57th Street house and went into the real estate business halfheartedly. Then he met Anna Rebecca Hall. The Halls were descended from the landed Livingstons and Ludlows, whose property on the Hudson was deeded to the Livingston family by three different English kings.

Anna, almost nineteen and the eldest of four sisters, was considered the leading debutante that winter. The four siblings were beautiful "society belles, and all were considered slightly but attractively mad. Anna was the most competent, and she was also a little cold," Franklin and Eleanor Roosevelt biographer Joseph Lash wrote. The couple became engaged on Memorial Day 1883 and married on December 1 at Calvary Church, two blocks from Elliott's East 20th Street birthplace. The *New York Herald* described it as "one of the most brilliant social events of the season....The bride was every bit a queen."[165]

Eleanor Roosevelt in 1889. *Courtesy of the Franklin D. Roosevelt Library.*

The couple moved into a brownstone at 29 East 38th Street, and Elliott went to work for the Ludlows' real estate firm, the most prominent in the city. "Anna and Elliott belonged. They and their friends set the fashion in dress and manners," Lash wrote. On October 11, 1884, at their brownstone, Elliott and Anna celebrated the birth of their first child, who was named Anna after her mother and Bamie, their favorite sister and sister-in-law, and Eleanor after her father, who had been called Ellie as a child. Eleanor was educated by a private tutor in the upper floor of their house, which was turned into a schoolroom for children of Anna's friends.[166]

In 1887, after a six-month trip to Europe, the family lived at 56 West 37th Street. When she was around four, Eleanor's daily ritual was to tiptoe into her adored father's bedroom to make sure that he was up and if he was still in bed to warn him that he was late for breakfast. In 1888, Elliott arranged for a large home to be built on ten acres in what is today Westbury on Long Island so he could devote more time to polo and hunting. Eleanor got a brother, Elliott Jr., on October 1, 1889. Another sibling, Hall, was born a year and a half later.[167]

After the family traveled to Italy in the winter of 1890, Anna moved into a house in a suburb of Paris. Meanwhile, Elliott entered a sanitarium to deal with his alcoholism while Eleanor was sent to a convent to learn French. When they returned to America that fall, Anna bought a house at 52 East 61st Street, two blocks from Bamie's home.[168]

When her mother contracted diphtheria while her father was in "exile" in Virginia because of his alcoholism, "suddenly everything was changed!

We children were sent out of the house," Eleanor wrote in *The Autobiography of Eleanor Roosevelt*. She went to stay with her godmother, Susan Parrish. Anna had entered the hospital for unexplained surgery and then, after the operation, contracted diphtheria and died at the age of twenty-nine on December 7, 1892. In her will, Anna had asked that her children be raised by her mother, Mary Hall, with her brother-in-law Theodore as legal guardian. So Eleanor and her brothers went to live with Grandmother Hall in her gloomy Manhattan brownstone at 11 West 37th Street.[169]

"As I look back on that household in the 37th Street house," Eleanor wrote, "our old-fashioned, brownstone house was much like all the other houses in the side streets, fairly large and comfortable, with high ceilings, a dark basement, and inadequate servants quarters with working conditions which no one with any social conscience would tolerate today. The laundry had one little window opening on the backyard and, of course we had no electric light. We were modern in that we had gas! The servants room lacked ventilation and comfortable furnishings. Their bathroom was in the cellar, so each one had a basin and a pitcher in a tiny bedroom. Our household consisted of a cook, a butler, a housemaid—who was maid as well to my young aunts and a laundress." There was a drawing room "with this massive gilt furniture covered with blue damask," a library in the front of the house with a piano and a large bow window. The dining room was in the extension in the rear with bright light entering from three windows on the side. Behind that was a pantry where the butler, Victor, taught Eleanor how to wash and dry dishes. The eccentric household consisted of Grandmother Hall and two uncles and two aunts. Eleanor added to the total with her two little brothers and their nurse.

Grandma Hall was convinced that Eleanor was developing curvature of the spine, so for nearly a year she had to wear an uncomfortable steel brace that prevented her from bending over. Eleanor took piano lessons and attended a fashionable dance school, which she hated because of her looks, her skinny tall frame and the unfashionable clothes that her grandmother insisted she wear.[170]

In the spring after her mother died, just before her eighth birthday, Eleanor was sent to stay with relatives after both of her brothers contracted scarlet fever. Baby Hall recovered, but three-year-old Elliott Jr. developed diphtheria and died of the same disease that had killed his mother.[171]

Elliott, deteriorating quickly from his unstoppable binge drinking, leased a townhouse at 313 West 102nd Street under the name of "Mr. Eliot."

Elliott Roosevelt lived at 313 West 102nd Street east of Riverside Drive when he was forced to stay away from his family because of his alcoholism until his death on August 14, 1894. *Author photo.*

After showing up sporadically in Eleanor's life, he had to be reminded by his sister Corinne that he had agreed to refrain from such visits "for the sake of the children."[172]

Elliott moved to Abingdon, Virginia. Just before her tenth birthday, Eleanor learned from her mother's younger sisters, Edith (nicknamed "Pussie") and Maude, that her father at age thirty-four had died after attempting suicide by jumping out of a window. He survived the fall but suffered a seizure and died on August 14, 1894, in Abingdon. He was buried in Brooklyn's Green-Wood Cemetery with none of his children, siblings or other close relatives in attendance.[173]

Now an orphan, Eleanor lived on the noisier street side on the fourth floor of her grandmother's brownstone. "I've always lived in other people's houses," she said later. "I always had to take the worst room." Grandma Hall maintained a stiflingly rigid household at 11 West 37th Street. Before breakfast every morning, the entire household, including servants, met for prayers in the dining room. On Sundays, Eleanor recited to her grandmother in French and instructed the coachman's small daughter in Bible studies. Twice daily she was compelled to improve her posture by walking back and forth holding a stick through her arms and behind her back. Her only relief was long afternoon walks with a series of French and German nannies.[174]

Life changed for Eleanor when her grandmother decided that the girl of fifteen should be educated in Europe as her mother had wanted. So in the fall of 1899, she sailed for England with the family of her Aunt Pussie Mortimer. Eleanor was enrolled in Allenswood, a school a short distance outside London, at the urging of her Aunt Bamie. When Eleanor turned eighteen, her grandmother decided it was time for her to come home for good to "come out" or be presented to society. She lived with her grandmother upstate and in the city with Henry and "Cousin Susie" Parish on East 76th Street. It was a twin house with one entrance into the home of Mrs. E. Livingston Ludlow, cousin Susie's mother and Grandma Hall's sister, and the other into the home of the Parishes.[175]

"Poor Eleanor!" her sharp-tongued cousin Alice Roosevelt Longworth commented about her. "She had a miserable childhood, which I don't think she ever got over."[176]

BAMIE

Three months after the death of their mother, Bamie, the oldest of the four children, purchased a brownstone at 422 Madison Avenue between 48th and 49th Streets. Theodore's young daughter Alice lived there with her while he finished his term in the state assembly and then dealt with his grief over the death of his wife and mother by heading out to live on his ranches in the Dakota Territory.

In 1886, shortly after Alice turned two, Bamie spent $50,000 from her share of the sale proceeds from the West 57th Street house on a new home at 689 Madison Avenue near 62nd Street. She lived there until moving to England in 1893 after the wife of her cousin James Roosevelt, Helen Astor, died, and she lived with him for two years to help take care of his two teenage children.

While in England, in 1895, she married divorced U.S. Navy Rear Admiral William Sheffield Cowles. The couple returned to America and owned a home in Washington, D.C., where Bamie entertained important people at what was known as the "other White House." They also purchased a house in Farmington, Connecticut, where she died in 1931.[177]

THEODORE

As much as she loved taking care of her brother's baby daughter, Bamie told TR that Alice needed a permanent home. So, two weeks after the death of his mother and his wife in 1884, Theodore signed a contract for construction of a Queen Anne–style house on his property on Long Island, which had once been occupied by Native Americans. But now the house would be called Sagamore Hill for a Native American sagamore or chief who had lived there rather than Leeholm for his wife.[178]

While Theodore finished his assembly term in Albany and worked on his ranches in the Dakota Territory, Bamie took care of young Alice at her brownstone at 422 Madison Avenue. TR would stay there when he visited New York. His older sister also oversaw construction of the new home in Cove Neck. Theodore began living at Sagamore Hill when he was in the East beginning at the end of June 1885. He left the Dakotas for good in the fall of 1886.

On one of his trips home in the fall of 1885, TR ran into old family friend Edith Carow as he was entering Bamie's house. They had not seen each other in nearly two years; she had kept her distance after the wedding. They rekindled their mutual interest, and in the spring of 1886, Edith sailed for England for an extended visit with her mother and sister. Roosevelt decided to meet Edith there and secretly marry her in London on December 2, 1886. Because it was so soon after Alice's death, Bamie and Corinne were scandalized. When the couple returned to America in March 1887 after honeymooning in Europe, they moved into Sagamore Hill.[179]

Finally, all four of the Roosevelt siblings each had a home of their own.

And, interestingly, thirty-seven years later, the house where they had been born on East 20th Street would be re-created.

7
THE RESURRECTION OF THEODORE ROOSEVELT BIRTHPLACE

After the death of Theodore Roosevelt in January 1919, a group of female admirers formed the Women's Roosevelt Memorial Association (WRMA). Even though the organization was formed by women, it chose a man, William Loeb Jr., TR's former secretary, as its first president.

The constitution of the association, initially based in Oyster Bay, Long Island, the location of Theodore Roosevelt's Sagamore Hill home, was adopted in January 1919. It stated that the purpose of the group, which later changed its name to the Women's Theodore Roosevelt Association, was "to found, erect and maintain, a suitable and enduring memorial to the late Honorable Theodore Roosevelt."[180] The WRMA was incorporated by an act of Congress on May 31, 1920. The bill stated that "the purpose of this corporation shall be to perpetuate the memory of Theodore Roosevelt for the benefit of the people of the United States of America and of the world." The bill specified that the goals of the association were "the erection and maintenance of a suitable and adequate monumental memorial in the city of Washington" and "the acquisition, development, and maintenance of a public park in memory of Theodore Roosevelt in the town of Oyster Bay, New York." There was no mention of acquiring Sagamore Hill or the East 20th Street property to rebuild Theodore Roosevelt's Birthplace.[181]

The reconstruction of Theodore Roosevelt Birthplace. *National Park Service—Theodore Roosevelt Birthplace NHS.*

The WRMA would cooperate with a men's group with a similar purpose, the Roosevelt Memorial Association, which in 1953 became the Theodore Roosevelt Association. The organizations, which would officially merge in 1955, acquired land for a public park in the middle of the Potomac River in Washington, D.C. They obtained land for Theodore Roosevelt Memorial Park in Oyster Bay. They purchased Sagamore Hill from the Roosevelt family after the death of former First Lady Edith Roosevelt, and they rebuilt the birthplace and adjoining brownstone of Robert B. Roosevelt in New York City.

After acquiring the two properties on East 20th Street by the end of 1919, the WRMA hired Theodate Pope Riddle (1867–1946), a philanthropist from Ohio who was one of the first female American architects, to oversee the project of erecting replicas of the structures. Riddle, a survivor of the sinking of the RMS *Lusitania* during World War I, wanted to focus the public's attention on the re-created birthplace. So when Robert's house next door at 26 West 20th Street was rebuilt, she gave it a blank façade, Daniel Prebutt, the National Park Service curator for Manhattan historic sites, explained. Originally, both houses had identical façades.

By 1922, both brownstones had been reconstructed. The replica of the birthplace, called Theodore Roosevelt House at the time, was dedicated and opened as a museum on Theodore Roosevelt's birthday, October 27, 1923. The birthplace was interpreted as a museum house, appearing as it did during the time the family lived there while Robert's house was a library and museum displaying family artifacts.

In its 1924 annual report, the Theodore Roosevelt Association reported:

The dining room at reconstructed Theodore Roosevelt Birthplace about 1923. These pieces of furniture are among the oldest in the house. The set dates from the early 1800s and was previously used by TR's grandfather Cornelius Van Schaack Roosevelt in his home on Union Square. *Library of Congress.*

A year ago Roosevelt House was opened to the public. It is a cheerful duty to report that any fears which some of the trustees may have felt that the proximity of the officers and staff of the Roosevelt Memorial Association and the officers and staff of the Woman's Roosevelt Memorial Association under one roof might cause friction, have not been realized. The relations of the two Associations are in every way admirable. A spirit of real cooperation has developed. There is no sense of rivalry…for the two Associations served together, as partners. The appropriations which the Roosevelt Memorial Association has made towards the completion of Roosevelt House and the installation of the collections, amounting in all to $182,000, have thoroughly justified themselves. During the year, 30,000 visitors have come to the House, many of them children from the schools of Greater New York, and some eighty meetings have been held in the auditorium [on the top floor of the library-museum building]. *The House is slowly becoming known and it is not improbable that before*

The auditorium at Theodore Roosevelt Birthplace in 1923. *National Park Service—Theodore Roosevelt Birthplace NHS.*

many years it will become for adults and children alike the most popular of the city's historical shrines.

The collections both in the library and the museum were constantly growing. The number of items in the library alone, including manuscripts, letters, books, pamphlets, clippings, cartoons and photographs, was 23,168.

Valuable gifts and temporary or permanent loans are constantly being received. Mrs. Roosevelt has been particularly generous and has contributed memorabilia of various sorts and of priceless value. The most striking addition to the museum during the past year is a bronze statue of Colonel Roosevelt as a Rough Rider, a replica in reduced size of an heroic statue which the donor, Dr. Henry Waldo Coe, presented to the city of Portland, Oregon. It was unveiled with due ceremony on May 25, by Colonel Roosevelt's granddaughter, Belle Wyatt Roosevelt.

WRMA's staff included a director, his secretary, an accountant, a stenographer and an office boy working at the organization's headquarters, now located at the Metropolitan Tower at 1 Madison Avenue. A librarian, his secretary, an assistant librarian, a motion picture expert, a part-time telephone operator and an office assistant worked at Roosevelt House. The WRMA also employed a librarian and a cataloger at the Library of Congress as well as an archivist at Harvard. The associations donated many documents and photographs to both institutions. On June 1, 1925, the association headquarters was relocated from Madison Avenue to Roosevelt House.[182]

The annual report for 1925 stated that

Roosevelt House has had an active year. About 130 meetings were held in the auditorium, half of them or more gatherings of school-children.…During the past twelve months 21,559 persons visited the House, representing every State and every important city in the Union, besides Alaska, Hawaii and the Philippines, and thirty-four foreign countries, including Canada, England, Ireland, Scotland, Wales, France, Germany, Italy, Greece, Armenia, Bulgaria, Norway, Sweden, Denmark, Mexico, Brazil, Iceland, Belgium, Holland, Finland, Switzerland, Hungary, Cuba, Bermuda, China, Japan, Korea, Australia, New Zealand, Tasmania, India, Bolivia, Gold Coast (Africa), Orange Free State (Africa). The WRMA's share of the cost of operating the house

> *during the past year was $5,469.77. The management of the House, under the general direction of Mrs. Alexander Lambert, chairman of the House Committee, is most notably efficient and economical.*[183]

The annual report for 1926 noted that "the work of Roosevelt House… shows a steady growth from year to year, as the birthplace becomes known to a wider circle, and as the civic activities which have their center there enlist the sympathy and co-operation of new friends of the good cause." During the year, 24,674 persons visited, an increase of about 3,000, including 8,361 schoolchildren.

Visitors included Emily Carow Tyler, sister of Edith Roosevelt, Alice Roosevelt Longworth, TR's elder daughter; and Ethel Roosevelt Derby, Alice's younger sister. Less celebrated visitors came from nearly every country in Europe, China, Japan, India, Burma, South Africa, Canada, Australia, South America, Haiti, Colombia, Guatemala and Mexico. About 204 meetings were held in the auditorium, an increase of 74 over the previous year. "Most of these meetings were arranged for schoolchildren; there is therefore a healthy growth in the field where the House can unquestionably render its most effective service. There has been a marked increase also in the attendance of foreign-born adults, for whom special meetings have been arranged. No visitors to the House show more earnest appreciation of the significance."[184]

On May 21, 1953, Congress approved the name change from the Roosevelt Memorial Association to the Theodore Roosevelt Association at the request of the organization to eliminate confusion over its purpose.[185]

In a report to Congress reprinted in the *Congressional Record* in June 1955, the TRA on its thirty-fifth anniversary summarized its history and reported on progress toward its goals. The organization noted that prior to its incorporation, there was a nonpartisan group known as the Roosevelt Permanent Memorial National Committee headquartered in New York City, which after a nationwide campaign had received contributions totaling $2,049,164.49. Acting on the recommendation of a committee headed by Elihu Root, TR's secretary of state, and James R. Garfield, his secretary of the interior, the associations purchased at a cost of $364,000 a ninety-acre island in the Potomac River and presented it to the nation as "a natural park for the enjoyment and recreation of the people" that would be developed by landscape architect Frederick Law Olmsted. The associations established a memorial park on the waterfront in Oyster Bay and in 1942 presented it to the Town of Oyster Bay at a cost of $850,000. The RMA also contributed

$165,000 to the completion of Theodore Roosevelt House. Immediately following the death of Edith Roosevelt in 1948, the RMA purchased Sagamore Hill and its furnishings. It had also gathered an extensive collection of books and pamphlets by and about Theodore Roosevelt, which were donated to Harvard University in 1943. "Plans for the expansion of the work in behalf of responsible citizenship are now being prepared in order that Theodore Roosevelt House may play an increasingly effective part in the life of the city and the Nation," the report said.[186]

An undated TRA membership pamphlet from the 1970s noted the spending by the women's and men's organizations: reconstruction of Theodore Roosevelt Birthplace, $540,000; Roosevelt Memorial Park purchased in 1925, $800,000; and purchase and restoration of Sagamore Hill, 1948–1953, $400,000.[187]

The TRA opened Sagamore Hill as a museum on June 14, 1953, with President Dwight D. Eisenhower, former President Herbert Hoover and New York Governor Thomas Dewey on hand to dedicate the house as a shrine. The *New York Times* reported on its front page that about 10,000 people attended. But while the TRA was charging admission at both the Birthplace and Sagamore Hill and enjoying substantial visitation, it also realized by the end of the 1950s it still was losing money running the properties and would go bankrupt if it did not take drastic action. The minutes of the forty-fourth annual meeting of the TRA board on October 23, 1962, reported that in the past year admissions had netted $1,747 and sales had amounted to $1,574 and there had been 4,296 children visiting. It did not detail expenditures. To deal with the rising cost of running the two properties, the association decided to approach the National Park Service about assuming ownership of the birthplace and Sagamore Hill.[188]

8
THE NATIONAL PARK SERVICE TAKES OVER THE BIRTHPLACE

To deal with the crippling costs of operating Theodore Roosevelt Birthplace and Sagamore Hill, the Theodore Roosevelt Association approached the federal government in the early 1960s about having the National Park Service take over the two sites. To sweeten the deal, the TRA offered to provide a $500,000 endowment.

In response, Secretary of the Interior Stewart L. Udall visited New York and liked what he saw. Legislation was introduced in Congress to implement the acquisition, and on April 2, 1962, the House of Representatives unanimously passed the bill to accept the properties. Senate approval followed on July 18. The legislation was sent to President John F. Kennedy, who signed the bill on July 21. Udall accepted the deeds, and the two properties became the park service's seventeenth and eighteenth national historic sites.[189]

The association provided a bill of sale that noted all the objects in the houses that were being transferred to the park service. Among the original objects at the birthplace were the following:

First Floor

The Parlor: The only artifact original to the house in this room is the lead crystal chandelier that came from Roosevelt & Son at 94 Maiden Lane.

THE LIBRARY: All of the books are from the Roosevelt family collection, including one of young Theodore's favorites, *Wood's Illustrated Natural History* by the Reverend J.G. Wood. The obelisks were brought back from the family's trip to Egypt in 1872. The table lamp came from Roosevelt & Son.

THE DINING ROOM: The set of table and chairs was brought to the house after it was initially used in the home of Theodore Sr.'s father, Cornelius Van Schaack Roosevelt, on Union Square. When Theodore Sr. and Mittie married, CVS gave them not only the house on 20th Street but the dining room set as well. The sideboard is original. When the Woman's Roosevelt Memorial Association opened the house as a museum in 1923, the organization did not have a set of china to display in the dining room, according to Daniel Prebutt, curator of the park service's Manhattan sites. "Members of the Roosevelt family did not want to part with their china, which is understandable, because it's a family heirloom," he told the author. "So Eleanor Roosevelt was very nice and went out and found a similar set, similar design, same time period, and she donated it to the museum. Although it is not original, the fact that Eleanor went out and got it just for the museum is a really wonderful story." Descendants of TR did donate one plate of family chinaware that is displayed on the mantel.

SECOND FLOOR

MASTER BEDROOM: "The whole bedroom set is original to the house," Prebutt said. "It is not the bed on which any of the Roosevelt children were born. Nobody knows where that bed went. The bedroom set was acquired near the end of their residency in the house, and it was the one extravagant purchase that Theodore Sr. made. It's a matching bedroom set with a bed, dresser, armoire, nightstand, secretary desk and two chairs made out of satinwood with rosewood trim. He paid $3,500 for it about 1870. That is about $84,000 now."

THE NURSERY: The original black walnut crib used by TR is on loan from the Palfrey family, descendants of his son Kermit. The child's rocking chair is also original to the house. The black walnut sleigh bed was where Mittie's sister Anna Bullock slept when she was the children's governess. Over the mantel are two embroidery samplers, one made by Anna Bullock in 1842 and the other by Edith Carow's mother, Laura F. Carow, in 1837.

The museum on the ground floor of the re-creation of Robert B. Roosevelt's house contains many artifacts from TR's life. The most dramatic are the bloodstained shirt he was wearing when he was shot in the chest in Milwaukee during the 1912 Progressive Party presidential campaign and the metal eyeglass case and folded speech that were in his pocket and saved his life.

Despite increased interest in Theodore Roosevelt in recent years from biographies and documentaries, the Birthplace remains one of the lesser-known New York City tourist attractions. It is visited by up to twenty-six thousand people a year.

At the beginning of 2025, several projects were in the works at the site. According to North District Ranger Callie Tominsky, cosmetic repairs were being completed in the auditorium so it could be reopened for use. The staff was also developing a new exhibit expected to open by late 2025 to detail how the house and neighborhood informed TR's upbringing and offer perspectives of the working class of New York at the time.

9

SARA, FRANKLIN AND ELEANOR ROOSEVELT

Two original Roosevelt family homes—both houses where Franklin and Eleanor Roosevelt lived—survive in Manhattan.

One is a brownstone at 125 East 36th Street known as the Draper House in the Murray Hill neighborhood that Sara Delano Roosevelt rented for her son and daughter-in-law after their marriage. The more prominent home is one now called Roosevelt House, the connected townhouses where Sara, Franklin and Eleanor lived until FDR and Eleanor moved into the White House in 1933. Thanks to Hunter College and one of its presidents with a major commitment to preservation, it survives on East 65th Street.

After Franklin Delano Roosevelt married Anna Eleanor Roosevelt, his fifth cousin once removed, in 1905, his mother rented them a Manhattan home. Since she doted on her only child, that place was near her own residence. And when Sara decided the couple needed more space for their growing family, she arranged that it should not only be adjacent to—but also connected to—a new home for her on East 65th Street.

Sara Delano

Sara was the daughter of Warren Delano. The Delanos were wealthier than the Roosevelts and had better bloodlines as well. The first Delano, then spelled "De la Noy," was Philip, who landed at Plymouth in 1621, a year after the *Mayflower* arrived and before the first Roosevelt immigrant.[190]

The early Delanos, whose family compound still exists in Fairhaven, Massachusetts, were merchants and ship captains. They included Ephraim in the mid-eighteenth century and Captain Warren Delano, twice captured by the British navy during the War of 1812. Warren Delano Jr. greatly boosted the family fortune through the opium trade, allowing him to purchase large homes along the Hudson River. Warren knew that to further succeed financially and socially, the Delanos needed to live in Manhattan. He moved the family into an elaborate townhouse at LaGrange Terrace and Lafayette Street. They lived next to his younger brother Franklin Hughes Delano, who had married Laura Vanderbilt several years before. Their other neighbors included Vanderbilts, Astors and writer Washington Irving in a complex of buildings now known as Colonnade Row south of Astor Place. The Greek Revival building originally contained nine townhouses built between 1830 and 1832. Each was twenty-seven feet wide with twenty-six rooms, and the townhouses were all interconnected. Today, only four townhouses remain: numbers 428, 430, 432 and 434, all New York City landmarks also listed on the National Register of Historic Places.[191]

Early photograph of LaGrange Terrace in Greenwich Village. *New York Public Library.*

Sara's father, Warren, was an avid Republican who had amassed a fortune from trading in China, where he had moved at the age of twenty-four. When he returned to America in 1843, the thirty-three-year-old bachelor met eighteen-year-old Catherine Lyman, who was from a well-connected but not wealthy family. The couple married and moved to China. The Delanos returned to New York in 1846 and bought a house at 39 Lafayette Place just east of Washington Square. The Delanos also owned a country estate, Algonac, about seventy-five miles up the Hudson River near Newburgh. Sara was born there in September 1854, Catherine Delano's seventh child.[192]

As a young girl, Sara lived in Hong Kong for two years when her father returned to China to work as a trader at the age of fifty after losing the fortune he had made on Wall Street. When Sara was ten, she was sent home with her siblings to live with their grandparents. After her parents returned to the United States shortly thereafter, the family was off on an extended European trip, and Sara attended school in France.[193]

Sara was known for her intellectual curiosity, evidenced by the fact that she had a stamp collection—a rare hobby for a female at the time—that coincided with her knowledge of geography from extensive travel. Her son, Franklin, would inherit that interest after he contracted polio, and it became a lifelong passion. By the time she reached adulthood, Sara, five-foot-ten with creamy skin and light brown hair, was considered one of the most beautiful women in New York. Her many admirers included architect Stanford White. Because Warren Delano did not like White, he sent Sara abroad.[194]

By 1871, when they were seventeen, Sara and Bamie Roosevelt had become close friends and were visiting each other frequently. Bamie became the matchmaker for her friend. Sara was twenty-six when in 1880 she married widower James Roosevelt, who was twice her age, at Algonac. James was a graduate of Union College who attended Harvard Law School before successfully devoting himself to investments that allowed him to live the life of the gentry at his one-thousand-acre Hyde Park estate called Springwood. James's first wife, Rebecca, whom he married in 1853, had died of a heart attack in August 1876. After a brief period of mourning, James began to court Bamie as a potential second wife. Despite her deformity and spinsterhood, Bamie gave James no encouragement. Instead, she arranged for him to meet Sara at a dinner she gave for them at her family's West 57th Street house. Four months later, they were married.[195] The marriage united two great Hudson Valley families but caused some astonishment in society because of the disparity in their ages.

"The Delanos were a fascinating family," Theodore Roosevelt's daughter Alice Roosevelt Longworth commented. "Much more so than the Roosevelts."[196]

Franklin D. Roosevelt with his father, James Roosevelt, in 1883, when FDR was sixteen months old. *Courtesy of the Franklin D. Roosevelt Library.*

FRANKLIN

After her marriage, Sara, who embraced her husband's Democratic politics, and James sailed for a European honeymoon in November on the *Germanic.* Elliott Roosevelt, on his way to India, was one of the passengers. When the couple returned to New York, Sara was four months pregnant. In January 1882, when Sara was twenty-seven, after being in labor for more than twenty-four hours, she gave birth at home to the couple's first and only child. He was named Franklin after Sara's uncle. In the spring after returning from India, Elliott was named Franklin's godfather.[197]

Like his distant cousin Theodore, Franklin was a sickly child. He contracted typhoid fever during a trip to London followed by chickenpox on a subsequent trip abroad. Until he entered Groton School in Connecticut at the age of fourteen, he studied at home with a private tutor like TR. The Oyster Bay Roosevelts considered him something of a sissy.[198]

Franklin D. Roosevelt's formal photograph taken at Groton School in Groton, Massachusetts, in 1900. *Courtesy of the Franklin D. Roosevelt Library.*

Franklin grew up sailing, birdwatching and accumulating specimens like TR. His mother, who doted on him, was overprotective and domineering. She sometimes invited local boys to come play with Franklin, but most of the time she was his only companion. In 1896, when Franklin went off to Groton at age fourteen, he arrived two years later than most boys because his mother was so reluctant to let him leave home. Nonetheless, he thrived before moving on in 1900 to Harvard. There he rowed on the crew team and spent most of his time working on the *Crimson* newspaper before completing his studies in three years. His father died on December 8, 1900, during Franklin's freshman year at Harvard, twenty years after marrying Sara. He left her comfortably wealthy.[199]

Eleanor

As described in chapter 6, Eleanor Roosevelt had a difficult and isolated childhood. Like Franklin, she was being tutored at home. Eleanor was shuttled between relatives because of her father's alcoholism and her mother's disdain for her. Both parents had hoped for a son. Nonetheless, Elliott doted on his daughter, but the beautiful Anna considered the future first lady solemn and ugly and so called her Granny.[200]

Eleanor and Franklin

Eleanor was sent to live with her maternal grandmother, Mary Hall, at her gloomy Manhattan brownstone at 11 West 37th Street after the death of her mother in 1892. Likely displeased with Elliott's drinking and scandalous behavior, Grandmother Hall mostly kept Eleanor away from any of the Oyster Bay Roosevelts. The one regular exception was at Christmas when she spent several days with her Aunt Corinne. "This was the only time in the year when I ever saw any boys of my own age," Eleanor wrote in her autobiography. "To me these parties were more pain than pleasure. The others all knew each other and saw each other often. They were all much better in winter sports….I was a poor dancer, and the climax of the party was a dance." Eleanor related that she "knew, of course, that I was different from all the other girls and if I had not known they were frank in telling me so! I still remember my gratitude at one of these parties to my cousin Franklin Roosevelt when he came and asked me to dance with him.[201]

Eleanor returned from her schooling at Allenswood outside London in 1902 after she turned eighteen because her grandmother decided it was time

Eleanor Roosevelt in her "coming out" portrait taken in New York City in 1902. *Courtesy of the Franklin D. Roosevelt Library.*

for her to "come out" as a debutante. Eleanor was one of five Roosevelt young women making their debut that year, and she was not looking forward to the ordeal. The event was the Assembly Ball held on December 11 at the old Waldorf hotel on 5th Avenue at 34th Street. "When the season of formal dances got underway, Eleanor's anxiety slicked her palms with sweat," biographer David Michaelis wrote. She never knew what to say. But when she was with fifth cousin Franklin, there were "no dreadful silences." Each time she saw him at events like the New York Horse Show or at dinners or dances, Franklin wanted to know which books she had been reading. "She realized that he, much like herself, was strangely at odds with the system, and that he needed her help."[202]

After the debutante ball, "Automatically my name was placed on everybody's list," Eleanor wrote in her autobiography. "I was asked to all kinds of parties." Because her Aunt Corinne had bought her clothes in Paris, "I imagine that I was well dressed, but there was absolutely nothing about me to attract anybody's attention. I was tall, but I did not dance well." Eleanor noted, "I had begun to see occasionally my cousin Franklin Roosevelt, who was at college…and various other members of his family and some of his college friends. His mother, Mrs. James Roosevelt, was sorry for me, I think."

When Eleanor was two years old, her parents had taken her to stay at Sara and James's house in Hyde Park. "My mother-in-law later told me she remembered…that Franklin rode me around the nursery on his back." But Eleanor's first recollection of Franklin was at one of her Aunt Corinne and Douglas Robinson's Christmas parties at their home in West Orange, New Jersey, in 1898 when she was fourteen. Later she caught "a glimpse of him the summer I came home from school" and was riding with family members on a New York Central train. "He spied me and took me to speak to his mother." Franklin had not written to Eleanor when she was in Allenswood. He referred to Eleanor only once in his letters from Harvard. But after their meeting on the train, his diary contained many references to Eleanor. "I never saw him again until he began to come to occasional dances the winter I came out and I was asked to a house party at Hyde Park," she wrote.[203]

"I had great curiosity about life and a desire to participate in every experience that might be the lot of a woman," Eleanor continued. "There seemed to me to be a necessity for hurry; without rhyme or reason I felt the urge to be a part of the stream of life, and so in the autumn of 1903, when Franklin…asked me to marry him, though I was only nineteen, it seemed entirely natural and I never even thought that we were both young and inexperienced." Franklin proposed during a weekend in Groton. When Eleanor returned home and her grandmother asked if she was sure that she was really in love, "I solemnly answered 'yes,' and yet I know now that it was years later before I understood what being in love or what loving really meant."[204]

While Franklin and Eleanor were in a hurry to have the wedding, Sara was not. "My mother-in-law had sense enough to realize that both of us were young and underdeveloped, and she decided to make her son think this matter over—which, at the time, of course, I resented." Sara took Franklin and a friend on a cruise to the West Indies that winter, but "Franklin's feelings did not change, however."[205]

In June 1904, Eleanor traveled with Sara to Franklin's Harvard commencement, and that summer she stayed with them at Campobello Island in New Brunswick, Canada. "We walked together, drove around the island, sailed on a small schooner with his mother and other friends, and got to know each other much better than ever before," she wrote.[206]

While waiting a year to announce their engagement in the fall of 1904, Eleanor joined the Consumers League to investigate conditions for low-income workers and volunteered with a friend at the Rivington Street Settlement House to teach immigrant children in keeping with the family tradition of assisting the poor. When once she allowed Franklin to visit her at the settlement house, "all the little girls were tremendously interested."[207]

Franklin had considered a naval career, but his father urged him to go to law school instead so he would not be away from home so much. Franklin then planned to attend Harvard Law School but chose Columbia Law School instead to be closer to Eleanor. He began his studies in September 1904. After Franklin purchased a ring at Tiffany's, the couple announced their engagement at Thanksgiving and planned the wedding for the following spring. Eleanor's uncle Theodore sent his congratulations to Franklin, writing, "I am as fond of Eleanor as if she were my daughter."[208]

The president offered the White House as a wedding venue, but Franklin and Eleanor preferred to marry in New York.

While Franklin studied at Columbia Law, Eleanor wrote in her autobiography, "his mother took a house at 200 Madison Avenue, and we had many gay times during the winter of 1905. Parties were given for us, wedding presents began to come, and my cousin Susie helped me to buy my trousseau and my linens. It was exciting and the wedding plans were complicated by the fact that Uncle Ted, at that time president of the United States, was coming to New York to give me away, and our date had to fit in with his plans. Finally, it was decided that we would be married on St. Patrick's Day, March 17, 1905, because Uncle Ted was coming on for the parade that day."[209]

"March 17 arrived," Eleanor continued. "Uncle Ted came to New York from Washington, he reviewed the parade, and then came to Cousin Susie's house," the Ludlow-Parrish house at 6–8 East 76th Street, the adjoining homes of Eleanor's cousin and godmother, Susan Parish, and her banker husband, Henry, and her mother, Mrs. E. Livingston Ludlow. Before two hundred guests, the president gave away the bride. Her twenty-one-year-old cousin Alice was the first of six bridesmaids. Eleanor asked the president's older daughter to stand in for Eleanor's deceased mother; it happened to be Anna's birthday. The bride wore her mother's heavy long-sleeved satin wedding dress, her Grandmother Hall's Belgian lace veil and a pearl necklace her mother-in-law purchased from Tiffany for $4,000, or more than $100,000 in current value. After Eleanor handed her bouquet of lilies to Alice, the ceremony was performed by the Reverend Endicott Peabody, head of Groton School. A crowd outside shouted "We want Teddy!" so loudly that they occasionally drowned out Peabody. After the couple had kissed, TR turned to Franklin and said, "Well, Franklin, there's nothing like keeping the name in the family!"[210]

"My cousin Susie's drawing room opened into her mother's house, so it gave us two large rooms," Eleanor recollected in her autobiography. "We were actually married in Mrs. Ludlow's house, where an altar had been arranged in front of the fireplace....After the ceremony we turned around to receive congratulations from the various members of our families and from our friends. In the meantime, Uncle Ted went into the library where refreshments were served. Those closest to us did take time to wish us well, but the great majority of the guests were more interested in being able to see and listen to the President."[211] With almost everyone present ignoring Franklin and Eleanor in favor of the president, the

always acerbic Alice grumbled that "my father, who gave Eleanor away, lived up to his reputation of being the bride at every wedding and the corpse at every funeral and hogged the limelight unashamedly."[212] After "we left amidst the usual shower of rice," Eleanor wrote, the couple took a train to Hyde Park.[213]

The wedding united, at least temporarily, the Democratic Hyde Park Roosevelts with the Republican Oyster Bay Roosevelt branch led by the president. The next day, the *New York Times* reported on the event in its society pages:

A group of Columbia Law School students and their professors on the steps of Earl Hall in 1905. Franklin D. Roosevelt, a law student from 1904–7, is directly behind Professor Charles Terry, who is in the third row from the bottom, fifth from the left, with a bowler hat in his lap. *Law Library Special Collections at Columbia Law School.*

> *One of the most notable weddings of the year was…celebrated yesterday, when Miss Eleanor Roosevelt, daughter of the only brother of President Roosevelt and Franklin Delano Roosevelt, a cousin of the president, were married by the Rev. Endicott Peabody of Groton, Conn., at the residence of the bride's cousins, Mr. and Mrs. Henry Parish Jr.…The bride, walking with the president, and preceded by her six bridesmaids, came down the*

> *wide flight of stairs leading from the third floor to the second and across the large foyer hall at the rear of the Parish drawing room, through wide doorways and on to a large mantel at the west side of the Ludlow drawing room, where the ceremony took place.*

The wedding was such a major social event that the *Times* continued its coverage the following day: "The wedding of Miss Eleanor Roosevelt and Franklin Delano Roosevelt, her cousin, took the semblance of a National event. The presence of President Roosevelt…and the entire family and every degree of cousinship made it very much like a 'Royal alliance.'…The president is never so happy as when he is one of the chief actors at a great family gathering."

Eleanor and Franklin enjoyed a week by themselves at Springwood in Hyde Park before moving into a small apartment at the Webster Hotel at 40 West 45th Street "for the remainder of the spring while Franklin continued his study of law," Eleanor wrote. "It is not customary to have two honeymoons, but we did, because my husband had to finish out his year at law school."[214]

When Sara went to Hyde Park for the summer, Franklin and Eleanor moved into her house in Manhattan, "so I still did not have to display the depths of my ignorance as a housewife," Eleanor wrote. When Franklin finished his exams, the couple spent three and a half months in Europe and then returned for the fall semester. At their request, Sara rented a home for them at 125 East 36th Street known as the Draper House, located in today's Murray Hill Historic District. "She had furnished it and engaged our [three] servants," Eleanor wrote.

"I was beginning to be an entirely dependent person—no tickets to buy, no plans to make, someone always to decide everything for us," Eleanor continued. "A pleasant contrast to my former life, and I slipped into it with the greatest of ease. For the first year of my married life I was completely taken care of. My mother-in-law did everything for me." Eleanor left all of the arrangements for the new house to her mother-in-law except for a few minor requests: that their bedroom be painted white, the kitchen and basement whitewashed and that if a telephone was in the house it should remain there. Eleanor and Franklin put a stop to just one of Sara's plans—to spend a large amount of money to wire the house for electricity. Eleanor wrote from Paris that it was not worth spending the money because they planned to spend only two years in the house.[215]

When Eleanor landed in New York, she was feeling miserable. "I soon found out that there was a good reason, and it was quite a relief—for, little

Draper House today. *Author photo.*

idiot that I was, I had been seriously troubled for fear I would never have any children and my husband would be much disappointed," she wrote. She was pregnant and would be "perfectly miserable for three months before every one of my six babies arrived."[216]

Franklin called their new habitat their "fourteen-foot mansion." Two days after they moved in, he took makeup exams at the law school after his mother had sent his law books to London so he could study on his way home.[217]

Franklin and Eleanor would not live long in the fourteen-foot mansion, which still survives little changed, because Sara had a plan. But it was a plan with a catch.

10

THE DOUBLE TOWNHOUSE ON EAST 65TH STREET

The location of Franklin and Eleanor Roosevelt's 1905 wedding in the two connected Parrish-Ludlow homes provided inspiration for his mother's combined wedding and Christmas gift for the couple.

Sara Delano Roosevelt knew that the newlyweds' rented house would not suffice for long as their family grew. So she decided to build her own adjoining connected townhouses to provide the couple with more space while also keeping her physically and otherwise connected to them. The six-story structure would serve as the New York City home for three generations of Roosevelts until FDR and his family moved to the White House.

As noted in the previous chapter, when Eleanor and Franklin traveled to Europe for a belated honeymoon after he completed his term at Columbia Law School, Sara rented a house for them at 125 East 36th Street, furnished it and hired three servants. The couple's first child, Anna Eleanor Roosevelt, was born there on May 3, 1906. Once Eleanor was pregnant with James, who was born on December 23, 1907, her mother-in-law became even more concerned about the size of the couple's dwelling. When friends talked about it, "she could not resist whispering as loudly as possible: 'Too small!'"[218]

Ignoring whatever discomfort there might be for Franklin and particularly Eleanor, Sara unveiled her plans on Christmas Day 1906. She presented the couple with a small, rough drawing on her Hyde Park letterhead. It depicted a building with a flat roof, nine windows and smoke drifting from a chimney. Beneath it she wrote: "A Christmas present to Franklin & Eleanor from Mama. Number & Street not yet quite decided—19 or 20 feet wide."[219]

Besides wanting more room for Franklin and Eleanor and their children, Sara had another reason for wanting to leave her home at 200 Madison Avenue. "B. Altman's had come to the neighborhood, and in Sara's generation, when retail invaded, it was time to move uptown," Eleanor biographer David Michaelis wrote. (Theodore Roosevelt Sr. had made the same decision in 1871 when Broadway near his East 20th Street home had become overrun with department stores.) Always a person of action, Sara quickly purchased a pair of four-story houses built in the now-unpopular brownstone style in 1876 at 47 and 49 East 65th Street between Park and Madison Avenues for $79,000. She planned to replace them with a single large home for her, Franklin and Eleanor and their children. She hired Charles Platt, the architect who would later become famous for designing the Freer

Opposite: Eleanor and Franklin with James and Anna. *Courtesy of the Franklin D. Roosevelt Library*.

Above: Sara Delano Roosevelt's sketch she presented to Eleanor and Franklin at Christmas 1905 announcing her intention to build the double townhouse for herself and her son's family on East 65th Street. *Roosevelt House Public Policy Institute, Hunter College, CUNY*.

Gallery of Art in Washington. He had a well-established practice in New York City designing apartment houses and commercial buildings, one of them nearby on Lexington Avenue and 66th Street.[220]

Platt's plans for the thirty-five-foot-wide property completed in June 1907 depicted a six-story neo-Georgian buff brick-and-limestone building that would appear to be a single dwelling from the street. It would be accessible by climbing four steps from the sidewalk to a set of heavy wrought-iron doors. Once inside the vestibule, there were separate doors leading to the east and west side of the structure with the numbers 47 and 49 carved over their respective interior doorways. "Opening the iron-gated front entrance is like stepping into a Chinese box concealing two more front doors facing each other within," Michaelis wrote. Platt included elevators, which would prove invaluable after Franklin contracted polio. Sara approved the plans, which avoided having two separate façades squeezed into the narrow lot, and construction began. According to documents at the Franklin Delano Roosevelt Library at Hyde Park, buying the property, the design fees, demolition and construction of the new building cost Sara $247,000—the equivalent of more than $8 million today.[221]

Eleanor remarked that "the houses were narrow," but Platt had "made the most of every inch of space and built them so that the dining rooms and drawing rooms could be thrown together and made practically one big room."[222]

Platt's plans placed a reception room opening onto a central hall on the first floor of each residence with a stairway curving up along the inside wall. Going past the stairs and small hall with an elevator, service stairs and half bath, visitors would enter the dining room. The kitchen, pantry, other work areas and a staff sitting room were in the basement, and a subcellar contained coal and utilities. On the second floor, each home had a library at the front and a drawing room in the rear. The libraries featured built-in cabinets and fireplaces. The third and fourth floors each had two bedrooms with baths and closet-dressing rooms. A large light court between the two residences on the third floor allowed light into the hallways. Franklin and Eleanor's bedroom was on the third floor while the children had rooms on the third and fourth floors. Doors connected the front rooms on the fourth floor on both sides of the townhouse. The fifth and sixth floors were where the servants worked and lived. An open roof area behind the high parapet wall facing the street functioned as a drying space for laundry.

While the construction was underway, Franklin completed his three years of law study and passed the bar exam in the spring of 1907. He was hired as a law clerk, or "full-fledged office boy," as he put it, by the firm of Carter, Ledyard & Milburn located at 54 Wall Street.[223]

Eleanor noted that Sara's "husband had told her never to live with her children" because "it was intolerable to be dependent on them." Sara would not live with Eleanor and Franklin in theory, but in practice she almost did.[224] Eleanor wrote later in her autobiography,

> *My early dislike of any kind of scolding had developed now into a dislike for any kind of discussion and so, instead of taking an interest in these houses, one of which I was to live in, I left everything to my mother-in-law and my husband. I was growing dependent on my mother-in-law, requiring her help on almost every subject, and never thought of asking for anything that I thought would not be met with her approval. She was a very strong character, but because of her marriage to an older man she had disciplined herself into living his life and enjoying his belongings, and as a result she felt that young people should cater to older people. She gave great devotion to her own family and longed for their love and affection in return. She was somewhat jealous of anything that might mean a really deep attachment outside the family circle.*[225]

The Roosevelts moved into their new home, or homes, in 1908. Sara's was No. 47 on the western side of the structure while Franklin, Eleanor, Anna and James were in No. 49 on the eastern side. Eleanor's younger brother, Gracie Hall Roosevelt, also lived with them when he was not away at school or traveling.

As the intrusive Sara clearly intended, the adjacent homes were generally treated as a single unit. "Mirror-image parlors and libraries in the front of the house hinted at an understanding that the families would live separate existences," wrote historian Harold Holzer, the Jonathan F. Fenton director of the Roosevelt House Public Policy Institute at Hunter since 2015. "But in the rear of the building, those borders melted away. Sara made sure that retractable sliding doors united the two houses" at the dining rooms on the first floor and the parlors on the second floor.[226] Curtis Roosevelt, the eldest grandson of Franklin and Eleanor, said he did not differentiate between the two living spaces. "I went from one to the other without any sense of there being different houses."[227] He recalled once crossing over from one side to the other and realizing he did not know where he was or how to get back. Bursting into tears, he sat down and waited "to be rescued."[228]

"It was disorienting even for the adults to live this way," Michaelis wrote. For twenty-five years, Sara would often venture unannounced into the other side of the building, often at the least expected or wanted moments for Eleanor. "Mama might assert domination over the connecting doors, or she might suddenly appear on one of the two elevators, six stairways, or in any of one of twenty rooms, but her actual presence was not half so strange as the intangible sense of her *will* working its way into Eleanor's life through the house and its things."[229] Sara did let her daughter-in-law help pick out fixtures for their new home. But while she was unpacking when they moved into the house, Eleanor put her favorite blue vase on the brighter side of her dressing room mantel to make it more visible. A day or so later, she noticed it had been moved to the other side. Confirming that neither Franklin nor the servants had moved it, she moved it back only to find the next time she entered the room it had been shifted again.[230]

"Everyone out there who thought they had mother-in-law problems, this probably trumps anyone's story," Jennifer J. Raab, president of Hunter College, commented at a ceremony commemorating the seventy-fifth anniversary of Franklin and Eleanor Roosevelt's sale of the townhouse to the college.[231]

The stress caused by Sara's looming presence finally overwhelmed Eleanor. At one point, with two children under the age of three in the house and another on the way, Eleanor lost control and exhibited such fury that her cousin Helen Roosevelt Robinson was so alarmed that she called a doctor in fear that Eleanor would have a miscarriage.[232] In another episode, Eleanor wrote,

> *In the autumn of 1908 I did not know what was the matter with me, but I remember that a few weeks after we moved into the new house on East 65th Street I sat in front of my dressing table and wept, and when my bewildered young husband asked me what on earth was the matter with me, I said I did not like to live in a house which was not in any way mine, one that I had done nothing about and which did not represent the way I wanted to live. Being an eminently reasonable person, he thought I was quite mad and told me so gently, and said I should feel different in a little while and left me alone until I should become calmer. I pulled myself together and realized that I was acting like a little fool, but there was a great deal of truth in what I had said, for it was not developing any individual taste or initiative. I was simply absorbing the personalities of those about me and letting their tastes and interest dominate me.*[233]

"As always," Holzer noted, "Eleanor made do: her discontent with the living arrangements on East 65th Street may have helped motivate her to begin looking for fulfillment outside the home, a quest that would evolve into one the most consequential public service careers of any woman of the 20th century."[234]

Franklin and Eleanor never confronted Sara about her proper place in the townhouses or her relationship with her daughter-in-law for fear of antagonizing her. But occasionally, Franklin broached subjects he knew would be delicate.

The 1910 census showed that Franklin, Eleanor, Anna and James shared their 65th Street home with seven employees, all born in Europe. They included French butler Joseph Maillot, Irish cook Mary Ross, Norwegian nurse Mari Lund and Irish laundress Mary Carter. Sara on her side had three resident servants: butler Scott David Kay; his Swedish wife, Hedda Kay, who was the cook; and Irish maid Anna Morgan.[235] Franklin told his mother one day that he and Eleanor had arranged to have their servants live outside of the house, effective immediately. Aghast, Sara argued against it, and then when she saw that her son and daughter-in-law would not budge, Sara threw a fit. She then wrote to Eleanor about it but without any change in the couple's decision.[236]

Eleanor attempted to cope by using whatever time she had when not taking care of the children by trying to learn new things. She attempted to play golf at Campobello. "After days of practice I went out with my husband, and after watching me for a few minutes he remarked that he thought I might as well give it up!"[237] She took lessons to keep up with her French, German and Italian and did a lot of embroidery. On March 18, 1909, she gave birth to baby Franklin Jr., who died from heart failure on November 8. Elliott was born on East 65th Street on September 23, 1910. Franklin Delano Roosevelt Jr. arrived in 1914 and John Aspinwall Roosevelt in 1916.[238]

In the summer of 1909, Eleanor got a little breathing room from her mother-in-law when they returned to Campobello. Previously, they had stayed with Sara. But when the woman who lived next door to Sara's home died, she had stipulated in her will that Sara could purchase the house for the discounted price of $5,000 if it was for Franklin and his wife. Eleanor was overjoyed to be able to make her own decorating choices and invite whoever she wanted without getting her mother-in-law's approval. She wrote to her husband, "I have moved every room in the house around."[239]

11

THE TOWNHOUSE BECOMES A POLITICAL HEADQUARTERS

After passing the bar exam in 1907 and being hired as a clerk by Carter, Ledyard and Milburn, Franklin Roosevelt's interest shifted from practicing law to politics, just like Theodore Roosevelt.

A 1945 article in the *New Yorker* about Roosevelt's "office boy" days based on the recollection of one of his fellow clerks stated that "his political career was born at 54 Wall St." when Poughkeepsie lawyer John Mack began visiting the office to persuade Franklin to run for the state senate in 1910 in the heavily Republican Twenty-Sixth District. When Roosevelt decided to risk politics, he told his fellow-clerks about it and said that he was going to campaign in an automobile. He was one of the first to use an automobile to campaign."[240]

FDR's branch of the family and many other Roosevelts had been Democrats until the Civil War, when they became Republicans or "War Democrats" to support Abraham Lincoln in his effort to restore the Union. Later, most of them, including Theodore Roosevelt's uncle Robert and Franklin's father, James, reverted to being regular Democrats. But some, including Theodore Sr., remained Republicans.

"He was doing well" at the law firm, Eleanor wrote in her autobiography. "But Franklin had a desire for public service, partly encouraged by Uncle Ted's advice to all young men and partly by the glamour of Uncle Ted's example." In the 1910 race, "Franklin was conducting a novel campaign, for no one had ever before tried to visit every small four-corners store, every village in every town. He talked to practically every farmer and when the votes were counted that election day my husband was the first Democrat to win in thirty-two years. At the same time, through that first-hand contact with the people, he had learned much of their thinking and of their needs."[241]

After the election, Franklin and Eleanor rented their house at 49 East 65th Street to Elizabeth "Tissie" and Stanley Mortimer, Eleanor's aunt and uncle, and moved to State Street in Albany. While in the state capital, Franklin developed a friendship with a somewhat eccentric, disheveled, chain-smoking and indefatigable newspaper reporter named Louis McHenry Howe, who would play a major role in Franklin's ongoing political and personal life. In the winter of 1912, Eleanor and Franklin contracted typhoid fever. While FDR recovered in Manhattan, Howe, the "rather gnomelike little newspaperman from Albany, came to the rescue," Eleanor wrote. Howe accepted Franklin's request to run his reelection campaign and went to Dutchess County and won "for a man who was flat on his back at the time." After the election, the Roosevelts decided to live at their East 65th Street house and commute to Albany, where they would stay in two rooms at the Ten Eyck Hotel.[242]

Franklin moved to Washington in 1913 after Theodore Roosevelt, Eleanor's uncle, who had given her away at their wedding seven years earlier, lost a third-party attempt to regain the White House. TR's run as the Progressive Party candidate split the Republican vote with his handpicked successor, William Howard Taft, allowing Democrat Woodrow Wilson to defeat them both. Because of Franklin's support for Wilson, the president named FDR assistant secretary of the navy, the same post previously held by Franklin's distant relative Theodore Roosevelt, after the inauguration in March. Franklin resigned from the New York State Senate, and he and Eleanor rented their Manhattan house for part of their time in Washington to Thomas W. Lamont and his wife. Lamont, a Harvard College graduate like FDR, was a partner in J.P. Morgan

A family portrait taken in June 1919 in Washington, D.C. *Sitting, left to right*: FDR Jr., FDR, Eleanor, Sara and John; *standing*: Anna, James and Elliott. *Courtesy of the Franklin D. Roosevelt Library*.

& Company who also owned the *New York Evening Post.* While Franklin lived and worked in Washington, Eleanor and the children initially remained in Manhattan, spent the summer on Campobello Island and joined FDR in Washington in the fall.

FDR's seven-year tenure at the Navy Department was the last time before Franklin's presidency that the family was not living in the East 65th Street home his mother had built for them. While in Washington, Eleanor took a small step toward independence by learning people skills as a Red Cross manager during World War I.[243]

Lucy Mercer

Franklin and Eleanor's marriage was strained and came close to dissolving entirely during World War I. It was only saved because of negotiations that took place at the East 65th Street townhouse. At the recommendation of her Aunt Bamie, in December 1913 while Eleanor was pregnant again, she hired twenty-three-year-old Lucy Mercer as her part-time social secretary. With some people in Washington and members of the family gossiping about a possible affair between the attractive Lucy and Franklin, Eleanor fired Lucy on June 24, 1917. Five days later, Lucy was hired by the Navy Department under a new wartime clerical program. She was assigned immediately to the office of the assistant secretary of the navy. According to family lore, Eleanor threatened to leave Franklin if he did not get rid of Lucy. FDR resolved the problem by going to his boss and having him disband the clerical program. Lucy, after receiving a perfect performance report and a promotion, was abruptly discharged by "Special Order of Secretary of the Navy" with no explanation provided. But that failed to put an end to the Franklin-Eleanor-Lucy triangle problem.

As part of his government duties, Franklin sailed for Europe. On the way home from France, he contracted the Spanish flu on the USS *Leviathan*, and it evolved into double pneumonia. When Franklin arrived in New York in September 1918, an ambulance took him to Sara's side of the townhouse since his side was still being rented to the Lamonts. Eleanor decided to be useful as he lay in bed by unpacking his things from the trip. When she looked over the letters he brought back to help him catch up on his mail, she discovered love letters from Lucy. That brought the Lucy issue to a breaking point.

Franklin D. Roosevelt with his mother, Sara Delano Roosevelt; wife, Eleanor; and children at Campobello Island in 1920. *Courtesy of the Franklin D. Roosevelt Library.*

"Sara Delano Roosevelt had a morbid horror of divorce," Eleanor biographer David Michaelis wrote. "The rupture of a marriage signified the 'complete failure of a woman's life.'" Before any rash decisions were made, Sara convened a discussion with the couple on her side of the townhouse. She began by asking Eleanor what she intended to do. Family members later said Eleanor offered to give FDR "his freedom." Franklin replied: "Don't be a goose." Eleanor insisted her husband think about what he really wanted, and if he wanted Lucy, she would bow out. Sara knew she could not talk Franklin out of divorce if that's what he really wanted. But she wanted the marriage to continue because she knew Eleanor was vital to her son's future. Louis Howe served as mediator, shuttling back and forth between the others and convincing Franklin that his political future would be over if he split with his wife and did not listen to his mother, who still controlled the family's money. Franklin eventually apologized to his wife for hurting her and offered to give up Lucy for good. Eleanor insisted that Franklin must demonstrate that he still wanted Eleanor in his life, even if their relationship was going to be platonic. And so the marriage was saved.[244]

Eleanor's acid-tongued cousin Alice Roosevelt Longworth later remarked that "Eleanor never could cope with Franklin's romantic affairs, especially not with Lucy Mercer, who is the most serious of them all....Eleanor took the whole matter very seriously indeed and the relationship was never the same again."[245]

Eleanor hoped Franklin would take a break from politics after serving in the Wilson administration. But in June 1920, he traveled to San Francisco for the Democratic national convention to support the presidential nomination of New York Governor Alfred E. Smith. When the delegates compromised on the forty-fourth ballot by nominating Ohio Governor James M. Cox, they picked Franklin for vice president. In November, the Republican ticket of Warren Harding and Calvin Coolidge crushed the

Democrats with an electoral college vote of 404–212. Sara wrote in her datebook that "Franklin rather relieved not to be elected Vice President."[246]

Back at East 65th Street, Eleanor tried to figure out what to do. She took cooking lessons even though she had a cook, and she also studied shorthand and typing. Eleanor was rescued from her listlessness when she was invited to join the board of the New York League of Women Voters and headed its legislation committee.[247]

Franklin, meanwhile, was working at his law firm, Emmet, Marvin & Roosevelt, formed in 1920 and located at 52 Wall Street, during the day and spending his evenings making speeches to charity boards, civic groups and political clubs.[248]

In January 1921, while still retaining his partnership in the law firm, FDR was hired as a vice president and New York office manager of Fidelity & Deposit, a Maryland-based surety and bonding company. The welcome job offer came from an acquaintance and fellow sailor, Van Lear Black. A successful Baltimore businessman and newspaper publisher, Black was chairman of the Fidelity board. Roosevelt was to be in charge of the company's business in New York, New Jersey and New England and also have a seat on its board if he could successfully split his day. The arrangement called for FDR to devote his mornings to his law practice and the afternoons to Fidelity. FDR's generous salary for the part-time job was set at $25,000 (approximately $400,000 in current value).

Fidelity, founded in 1890, wanted to increase its business in New York, where it was already one of the four largest insurers in the surety and bond business. The companies offered surety bonds to cover losses if contracts were not fulfilled and fidelity bonds to protect companies and nonprofit organizations against losses incurred by financial misconduct of employees. When Roosevelt went to work at Fidelity's office in the prestigious six-year-old Equitable Building at 120 Broadway, he hired his loyal political advisor and former Navy Department assistant Louis Howe to join him. That decision would become critically important months later in 1921.[249]

Franklin's new boss Van Lear Black traveled from Baltimore to New York on his steam-powered yacht *Sabalo* at the end of July 1921. After FDR joined him aboard, they sailed to Campobello Island, arriving at the Roosevelts' summer home on August 7. Black and his party spent two days as the family's guests, with Eleanor reporting, "We were busy and spent the days on the water fishing and doing all we could to give them a pleasant time."[250]

Polio

After *Sabalo* had sailed away, FDR spent August 10, 1921, swimming, hiking and boating with his five children on Campobello Island. Late in the day, Roosevelt, then thirty-nine, complained of feeling tired but still took the children on a two-mile run to swim in a lake. When they returned, "he began to complain that he felt a chill and decided he would not eat supper with us but would go to bed and get thoroughly warm," Eleanor wrote in her autobiography. "The next day my husband felt less well. He had quite a temperature" of 103 degrees. "His legs became paralyzed and doctors diagnosed infantile paralysis or polio, as it was commonly described."[251]

It was decided to get Franklin to New York for treatment. He was transported by private railway car and spent a month in New York Presbyterian Hospital on East 68th Street. FDR returned home to 65th Street on October 28, 1921, and was carried to a quiet back bedroom on the third floor of the townhouse to continue his recuperation. Doctors, relatives, friends and other well-wishers came and went. But inquiring newspaper reporters were kept away, and details on Franklin's condition withheld to protect his future political career.

Soon FDR was reassuring friends and colleagues that "things are going very well, and at my present rate of progress it will not be many weeks before I am down at the office again." While Franklin had Howe handling day-to-day matters in the Fidelity office, Van Lear Black, Eleanor said, "was a warm friend and kept his place for him until he was well enough to resume his work."[252]

Sara, meanwhile, had "made up her mind that Franklin was going to be an invalid for the rest of his life and that he should retire to Hyde Park and live there," Eleanor wrote. "She always thought that she understood what was best, particularly where her child was concerned, regardless of what any doctor might say." But Eleanor, Howe and Franklin's doctor, George Draper (no relation to the Draper House mentioned earlier), felt strongly that FDR should continue to live and work in Manhattan to have any chance of a normal life rather than succumbing to what the Roosevelt children called their grandmother's "magnificent martyrdom."[253]

"Eleanor had her own ideas," wrote Harold Holzer, director of the Roosevelt House Public Policy Institute at Hunter College. "Franklin, she argued, should return to East 65th Street, where the elevator system would provide access not only within the multi-story dwelling but to the outside world."[254] In a rare instance of bucking his mother, Franklin agreed that they should stay in Manhattan. The only alterations made at 49 East 65th Street to accommodate FDR's condition was installation of an extra set of bronze handrails in the vestibule and portable wooden stairs with two railings placed over the front steps outside.[255] Franklin began a vigorous exercise program to strengthen his upper body. He also used a special armless wheelchair—"a little kitchen chair on wheels," Franklin called it—that could fit into the elevator and that he would use for the rest of his life.[256]

While Sara and Eleanor bickered over what was best for Franklin, he became so stressed over their disagreements that in the spring his doctors persuaded him to leave the house for a while for the relative quiet of Hyde Park. Meanwhile, with the Roosevelt children worried about their father, he did the best he could to reassure them. "He apparently knew it would be a shock for us to realize that the useless muscles in his legs would cause atrophy," daughter Anna recalled. "So father removed the sadness by showing us his legs. He gave us the names of each of the muscles in them, then told us which ones he was working hardest on at the moment. He would shout with glee over a little movement of a muscle that had been dormant....The battle Father was making became a spirited game." While he would never win the game of regaining use of his legs, FDR's ordeal taught him patience, determination and empathy that would serve him well in the future.[257]

It was not just Franklin's well-being that had made Eleanor push for the family to remain in Manhattan. To escape from the dominance of Sara and encouraged by Louis Howe, Eleanor had been branching out on her own. Even before her marriage, she had volunteered at a Lower East Side settlement house. And after women won the right to vote in 1920, she became active in civic organizations, first in the League of Women Voters, as mentioned earlier, and the Women's City Club. In addition, spurred by her husband's infidelity and with her marriage permanently strained, Eleanor wanted to pursue her own interests.

There was a break in the family's routine one day when Sara had just started to eat lunch at No. 47. A fire in the chimney was quickly extinguished by the servants. But the incident brought back painful memories for Sara, whose youngest sibling, Laura, then nineteen, had been fatally burned when an overturned alcohol lamp ignited her nightgown in 1884.[258] Even before the chimney fire, Franklin and his family worried about what would happen if his room was engulfed in fire. So one day he gathered the household in his bedroom and then showed how he could drop headfirst to the floor and use his elbows to drag his useless legs behind him to escape a fire. That demonstration prompted Eleanor to flee the room and weep.[259] According to James Roosevelt, FDR's oldest son, his father was terrified of being trapped in a fire or the house being consumed by flames. He wrote that "his helplessness did give Father one phobia, or rather intensified one that always bothered him—a fear of fire. Fire was the only thing I ever heard Father confess—either before or after polio—that he feared physically."[260]

That fear of fire may have been one of the reasons that FDR continually worked to strengthen his upper body using the gym apparatus in the house. He was assisted by a live-in nurse and Eleanor while plaster casts and wedges were used to painfully stretch his leg muscles to keep them from contracting. One day using wooden bars for balance, he shouted out for others to come look, proclaiming, "I can stand alone."[261]

Louis Howe, who was not only filling in for Franklin at work but also dealing with the press and other matters, moved into the front third-floor bedroom on weekdays to help out, returning to his family in Poughkeepsie on weekends. Sons Franklin Jr., born on August 17, 1914, at Campobello, and John Aspinwall, born on March 13, 1916, in Washington, and their nanny lived in fourth-floor bedrooms on Sara's side of the house. Even with older sons James and Elliott at boarding school, the house was so crowded that Eleanor later wrote that she "slept on a bed in one of the little boys' rooms. I dressed in my husband's bathroom. In the daytime I was too busy to need a room."[262]

Because of the strain, one afternoon in the fall of 1921, she wrote, "I suddenly found myself sobbing as I read" to her two youngest sons. "I could not think why I was sobbing, nor could I stop.…Finally I found an empty room in my mother-in-law's house, as she had moved to the country. I locked the door and poured cold water on a towel and mopped my face. Eventually I pulled myself together."[263]

Dr. Draper "felt strongly that it was better for Franklin to make an effort to take an active part in life again and lead, as far as possible, a normal life, with the interests that had always been his," Eleanor wrote.[264] So after a summer in Hyde Park, Franklin returned to work at Fidelity & Deposit's office at 120 Broadway. A chauffeur drove him between home and office. He relied on crutches and fourteen pounds of steel braces outside his suit pants to walk. One of the few times he slipped and fell in public was on the polished marble floors in the lobby at 120 Broadway, but he was quickly assisted back up. He eventually learned from a physical therapist to balance better on his braces by locking his arms and "walking" with an assistant. In his Fidelity office, he sat at a large walnut desk and reviewed the work of his

The desk FDR used at Fidelity & Deposit's office at 120 Broadway. *Author photo.*

staff and wrote letters to secure more business and stay in touch with friends and politicians around the country.[265]

Even though FDR was working again, Eleanor wrote that Howe "felt that one way to get my husband's interest aroused was to keep him as much as possible in contact with politics."[266] To do that, Howe urged her to get involved in political and civic work again, and she became active with the Democratic Party and the Women's Trade Union League. Eleanor organized gatherings of women political and social leaders in the linked dining and drawing rooms of the townhouse. One in 1924 was for representatives of the National Council of Women of the United States that Eleanor asked Sara to host. In attendance was Mary McLeod Bethune, president of the National Association of Colored Women, who would later become an advisor to FDR on African American issues during the New Deal. A friendship ensued, with Sara and Eleanor helping raise funds at the 65th Street home for what became Bethune-Cookman College in Daytona Beach, Florida, the institution where Bethune was president. Franklin, meanwhile, became president of the Boy Scout Foundation and chairman of the American Legion campaign and was involved in Harvard and other nonpolitical activities.[267]

Franklin's ongoing recovery effort was aided by his discovery in 1924 of the therapeutic benefits of the pools at Warm Springs in Georgia.[268]

Eleanor later wrote of her husband in the mid-1920s that "he was entirely well and lived a normal life, restricted only by his inability to walk. On the whole, his general physical condition improved year-by-year, until he was stronger in some ways than before his illness."[269] There were mental benefits

Sara Delano Roosevelt with educator Mary McLeod Bethune, director the Division of Negro Affairs for the National Youth Administration, during a visit to the East 65th Street townhouse. *Roosevelt House Public Policy Institute, Hunter College, CUNY.*

of coping with the polio for Eleanor as well as Franklin. "Both emerged from the ordeal tempered, tested and strengthened," biographer Joseph Lash wrote.[270]

Returning to Public Life

It would take Franklin three years to fully resume his public life. "In the spring of 1924, before the National Democratic Convention met in New York, Al Smith, who was a candidate for the presidential nomination, asked him to manage his preconvention campaign," Eleanor recalled. "This was the first time that my husband was to be in the public eye since his illness. A thousand and one little arrangements had to be made and Louis carefully planned each step of the way."[271]

To be able to nominate Smith at the convention, FDR increased his physical training so he could hold himself upright on steel leg braces and give the impression that he was walking to the platform while leaning on the arm of one of his sons. Using the braces and crutches, he practiced walking back and forth from the library to the parlor across the hall in the 65th Street house, which was about the same distance he would have to walk from the backstage area to the convention podium.[272] By the day of the convention, June 26, Roosevelt was able to make it to the podium to nominate the man he called the "Happy Warrior" without mishap while being greeted with cheers. FDR was able to give the impression that he had recovered from polio and could walk with assistance. Buoyed by his triumph—and despite Smith failing to win the nomination—Roosevelt began planning his political future from East 65th Street.[273]

In 1925, while still working at Fidelity, FDR became a partner in a new law firm. As noted previously, from 1920 to 1924 he was a partner at Emmet, Marvin & Roosevelt located on Wall Street. But FDR could no longer work in the firm's office after he contracted polio in 1921 because he was unable to climb the entrance stairs. Roosevelt, however, continued to be a partner in the firm for three more years. His second law firm was Roosevelt & O'Connor, which operated initially from 1925 to 1928 from a different floor than Fidelity at 120 Broadway. The firm existed until Roosevelt's inauguration as president in 1933. His partner was Basil O'Connor, a successful corporate lawyer who met Roosevelt in 1920 when he was running for vice president and became a lifelong friend and political advisor. O'Connor helped FDR buy Warm Springs in 1927. And he later assisted him in establishing the National Foundation for Infantile Paralysis—known popularly as the March of Dimes—in 1938 to raise money for research to find a cure for polio and care for those with the disease.[274]

Even though he was working at Fidelity and his law firm, "Franklin devoted a good part of his time to finding out how far he could recover from infantile paralysis," Eleanor wrote. "The use of his hands and arms came back completely and he developed, because he used them so constantly, broad shoulders and strong arms; but his legs remained useless. Little by little, through exercise and wearing braces, he learned to walk, first with crutches and then with a cane, leaning on someone's arm....However, for the rest of his life he was unable to walk or stand without the braces and some help."[275]

In the 1920s, Eleanor became involved in two enterprises with friends and political allies Nancy Cook and Marion Dickerman. Franklin helped design and build a stone cottage beside a brook on his Hyde Park property that was named Val-Kill after a nearby brook. The two women lived there, and Cook ran a furniture factory to provide jobs for local residents. Eleanor sold some of the furniture from the house on East 65th Street and held classes for women in the basement.[276] In 1922, Dickerman started teaching at the Todhunter School, a private college-preparatory school for upper-class girls founded by English-born Winifred Todhunter, an Oxford University graduate. In 1927, Dickerman, Cook and Eleanor purchased the school. Dickerman served as principal until 1937, while Eleanor was vice principal and teacher from 1927 to 1932 and remained associated with the school until 1938.

In 1928, when Al Smith sought the Democratic nomination for president a second time, he again chose FDR to give the nomination speech. Franklin told his oldest son, James, sixteen, to hold on to his left side while he used a cane on his stronger right side. He instructed James to engage him in laughing banter to disguise the fact that they were moving so slowly. Franklin again made it to the podium without mishap, although he was drenched in sweat. It was another triumph. After Smith was nominated on his second try, he and Democratic leaders persuaded FDR to run for governor of New York to replace Smith. Although Smith lost, FDR was elected.[277]

Eleanor Roosevelt displays a chair for sale in the parlor of her townhouse on East 65th Street around 1930. The furniture was made at Val-Kill, the Hyde Park furniture factory she founded with friends to employ local agricultural workers during the winter. *Roosevelt House Public Policy Institute, Hunter College, CUNY.*

RUNNING FOR PRESIDENT

The close relationship between Smith and Franklin cooled in 1932 when FDR was nominated to run for president instead of Smith as the Great Depression was devastating the economy. He and Eleanor voted at Hyde Park before quickly returning to East 65th Street to wait for the results. Winning easily over incumbent Herbert Hoover with a popular vote of 22.8 million to Hoover's 15.7 million, FDR addressed supporters at the Biltmore Hotel before returning to the townhouse at 1:40 a.m. His mother was waiting by the front door, and twenty-four years after building the home for her son's family and herself, she could greet him as president-elect. The *New York Times* reported that as Sara embraced him, FDR was overheard saying that "this is the greatest moment of my life."[278]

When the results were in, Eleanor wrote, "I was happy for my husband, because I knew that in many ways it would make up for the blow that fate had dealt him when he was stricken with infantile paralysis; and I had explicit confidence in his ability to help the country in a crisis....But for myself I was deeply troubled. As I saw it, this meant the end of any personal life of my own."[279]

After FDR had received President Herbert Hoover's concession telegram, he decided to address the nation by radio. On the day after the election, November 9, he was wheeled into the second-floor parlor on the east side of the townhouse and helped into an armchair before the fireplace. When he received a signal from a technician, Franklin began talking in conversational tones. He spoke for only about one minute, 153 words, rather than giving a speech. Across America, people in their own parlors listened raptly as their new president tried to allay their fears about the future:

> *I am glad of this opportunity to extend my deep appreciation to the electorate of this country which gave me yesterday such a great vote of confidence. It is a vote that had more than mere party significance; it transcended party lines, and became a national expression of liberal thought. It seems, I am sure, that the masses of the people of this nation firmly believe that there is great and actual possibility in an orderly recovery through a well-conceived and actively directed plan of action. Such a plan has been presented to you and you have expressed approval of it. This, my friends, is most reassuring to me. It shows that there is in this country unbounded confidence in the future of sound*

Sara, Franklin, James and Anna Roosevelt pose in front of the second-floor parlor fireplace in the East 65th Street townhouse on November 9, 1932, after FDR's radio broadcast following his election as president. *Courtesy of the Franklin D. Roosevelt Library.*

> *agriculture and of honorable industry. This clear mandate shall not be forgotten, and I pledge you this and I invite your help in the happy task of restoration.*[280]

"His voice lent itself remarkably to the radio," Eleanor wrote. "It was a natural gift, for in his whole life he had never had a lesson in diction or public speaking."[281]

After concluding his radio address, Roosevelt repeated it for the film cameras of Fox Movietone News, which put FDR's message on theater screens across the country within days. "Without leaving his own home, the incoming president had launched a communications revolution," Holzer wrote. That initial post-election talk began a series of live broadcasts that would continue when FDR arrived at the White House called "Fireside Chats."[282]

Transition Headquarters

After the 1932 election, Eleanor wrote, "Life began to change immediately.... The Secret Service assumed responsibility for his protection. Our house on 65th Street was filled with Secret Service agents, and guests were scrutinized and had to be identified when Franklin was in the house."[283]

For four months from Election Day until FDR's inauguration on March 4, the townhouse at 49 East 65th Street served as his official transition headquarters, just as it had served informally as his campaign headquarters. From his library, Roosevelt consulted with the advisors of his "Brain Trust," decided on his cabinet members and occasionally met with the reporters who gathered downstairs in the front reception area after Eleanor decided they should not have to stand outside in the cold.[284]

The most unusual of the cabinet appointees FDR selected was Frances Perkins as secretary of labor. He had decided early in 1933 to appoint the first woman to a presidential cabinet. Perkins, the New York State industrial commissioner, was a natural choice, having worked with Franklin for four years. She had first encountered FDR at a tea dance in Manhattan in 1910, when he had just entered politics to run for the state senate and she was working in a settlement house on a survey of social conditions in the neighborhood.[285]

On a morning in late February 1933, Perkins wrote in *The Roosevelt I Knew*, she received a call from Roosevelt's secretary asking her to come to 49 East

65th Street at eight o'clock that evening. When she arrived, she found that

In early 1932, Frances Perkins was offered the position of secretary of labor, making her the first female cabinet secretary in American history, by Franklin Delano Roosevelt in his library at East 65th Street after his election as president. *Library of Congress.*

> *the place was a shambles. Ever since the nomination six months before, a great many visitors, from cranks to persons destined to play important roles in the Roosevelt administration, had converged on the house for conferences or to seek favors from the President-elect. The press had established a base of operations on the first floor. The constant flow of visitors left the small staff of servants powerless to retain any semblance of order. Furniture was broken. Rugs were rolled up and piled in a corner. Overshoes and muddy rubbers were in a heap near the door. The floor was littered with newspapers. Trunks were jammed into one corner, and in another stood boxes containing Roosevelt's papers which had just been sent down from Albany and had to be sorted and filed for re-shipment to Washington. I made my way to the comfortable second floor where Roosevelt had his study. I was greeted by a secretary, who asked me to have a seat.*[286]

A stocky man with blond hair whom she did not know was sitting on a sofa and was brought into Roosevelt's study before Perkins. When she entered, Perkins was introduced to the man, Harold Ickes, who would become secretary of the interior. (Ickes and Perkins would be the only members of Roosevelt's cabinet to serve for his entire tenure in the White House.)

> *After Ickes left, Roosevelt came right to the point. "I've been thinking things over and I've decided I want you to be Secretary of Labor." His words came as no surprise to me. The newspapers had been speculating on this for days. Moreover, I knew that he wanted to establish the precedent of*

> *appointing a woman to his cabinet. Since the call from his secretary, I had been going over arguments to convince him that he should not appoint me. I led off with my chief argument, that I was not a bona fide labor person.... Roosevelt's answer was that it was time to consider all working people, organized and unorganized. I told him that it might be a good thing to have a woman in the cabinet if she were best for the job, but I thought a woman Secretary of Labor ought to be a labor woman. He replied that he had considered that and was going on my record as Industrial Commissioner of New York. He said he thought we could accomplish for the nation the things we had done for the state.*

Perkins realized that she was not getting anywhere with her argument and tried a different approach.

> *I said that if I accepted the position of Secretary of Labor I should want to do a great deal. I outlined a program of labor legislation and economic improvement....I thought that Roosevelt might consider it too ambitious to be undertaken when the United States was deep in depression and unemployment. In broad terms, I proposed immediate federal aid to the states for direct unemployment relief, an extensive program of public works, a study and approach to the establishment by federal law of minimum wages, maximum hours, true unemployment and old-age insurance, abolition of child labor, and the creation of a federal employment service. The program received Roosevelt's hearty endorsement, and he told me he wanted me to carry it out.*

Perkins then said that developing a package of these progressive and revolutionary social programs—which would become known collectively and famously as the New Deal—would require legislation that might be considered unconstitutional. "Well that's a problem," Roosevelt responded, "but we can work out something when the time comes." With that, Perkins wrote, "I agreed to become Secretary of Labor after a conversation that lasted but an hour."[287]

Franklin and Eleanor left East 65th Street at 4:00 p.m. on March 2, 1933, to travel to Washington for FDR's inauguration as the thirty-second president. They went by car to Liberty Street to board a special ferry to Jersey City and from there to take a train to the capital.[288]

After the inauguration, Eleanor frequently visited the townhouse to see Sara, but Franklin returned to East 65th Street only occasionally in the first

FDR and Eleanor leaving the East 65th Street townhouse for the White House in March 1933. *Courtesy of the Franklin D. Roosevelt Library*.

few years of his presidency. One of those visits, in late September 1933, was memorable for an image that resulted. FDR had stopped at the townhouse on his route to White Plains, and as he was leaving, the president held onto a special railing erected on the stairs, As he slowly made his way to the street, *Daily News* photographer Arthur Browne snapped a shot. But the newspaper never printed it because the image showed the steel braces emerging from FDR's pants cuffs down to his shoes. The newspapers at the time operated under a "gentlemen's agreement" that the press would never publish images that showed Roosevelt's disability. The picture was first published a half-century later.[289]

The Roosevelts came to New York for Memorial Day weekend in 1934 to review the U.S. Navy fleet from the heavy cruiser USS *Indianapolis*. They stayed at their 65th Street home, which was heavily guarded by police. "From the windows of neighboring houses and of Mayfair House, directly opposite No. 49, men and women hung out in hopes of catching a glimpse of the President on his return home," the *New York Times* reported on June 1.

"Private automobiles and taxicabs drove round and round the block, trying to coincide with the President's arrival, until at 5:15 the police barred traffic from the block."

FDR stayed again at his townhouse in January 1936. On the night of the eighteenth, he spoke from there in a telephone call that was also broadcast over the radio with the trustees of the Warm Springs Foundation, who were planning their annual fundraising ball to support the Georgia spa. The following day, the president and other members of the extended family drove through a blizzard to dedicate the Theodore Roosevelt Memorial at the American Museum of Natural History on Central Park West. FDR would also stay at the townhouse whenever he was in New York City for a political event.

Other members of his family lived in the 65th Street townhouse when Franklin was based in Albany and later in Washington. His daughter Anna, her husband, Curtis Dall, and their two children moved into the fourth floor on Sara's side in 1931 when they were forced to give up their home during the Great Depression. After Franklin and Eleanor moved into the White House in March 1933, Anna and her children (Anna, age six, and Curtis, age three) followed soon after while her husband remained in New York because they were separating. Franklin and Eleanor's oldest son, James, and his first wife, Betsey Cushing, used the townhouse in 1937.

But when Eleanor came to New York by herself, she usually stayed in a small walk-up apartment in Greenwich Village. She had spent a lot of time in that neighborhood with Esther Lape and her partner Elizabeth Read while Franklin was often at Warm Springs seeking relief from polio. In 1935, Lape and Read persuaded Eleanor to rent the third-floor apartment in their five-story brick building at 20 East 11th Street. She lived there from 1932 until 1942, as noted in a brass plaque near the door. It served as a sanctuary from the pressures of being first lady and allowed her to avoid dealing with her mother-in-law up on 65th Street.[290]

Eleanor had packed up a few of the family's possessions before moving to Washington in anticipation of renting their side of the 65th Street townhouse, but Franklin and Eleanor tried several times to rent No. 49 without success. The logical explanation was that any potential tenant would have to deal with Sara next door. The *New York Herald Tribune* reported on September 16, 1941, that "no tenant was ever found. One reason was that because of the close proximity to Mrs. James Roosevelt's residence, any prospective tenant had to be acceptable to her as a neighbor."[291]

After her son and Eleanor moved to the White House, Sara Delano Roosevelt continued to live at No. 47. When Sara's health began to decline, Eleanor gave up her Greenwich Village apartment in 1941 and stayed at No. 49 to help her mother-in-law. The two women moved up to Hyde Park in early September and were joined by Franklin before Sara died on September 7, 1941, two weeks before her eighty-seventh birthday. In her will, Sara left her New York City home to Eleanor and Franklin.[292]

Likely deciding that living on 65th Street after the death of his mother would bring unhappy memories and anticipating a post-presidential life at Hyde Park and elsewhere in Manhattan with their children grown, FDR quickly put the townhouse on the market for $60,000—about one-quarter of what his mother had invested in the property thirty-six years earlier. A "For Sale" sign was placed in front of the townhouse within a week of Sara's death.

The following spring, Eleanor returned to New York to clean out both sides of the townhouse. "We had lived in these houses since 1908 and one can imagine the accumulation of the years," she wrote in her autobiography. "My mother-in-law never threw anything away. It was a tremendous job."[293] Franklin and Eleanor signed a four-year lease for a seven-room apartment, 15A, at 29 Washington Square West, and Eleanor moved the family's New York City possessions there.[294]

Meanwhile, the townhouse remained on the market. Finding a buyer in the early days of World War II would be difficult. But with help from Eleanor and Franklin Roosevelt, a nearby college would buy and save it.

12
HUNTER COLLEGE ACQUIRES ROOSEVELT HOUSE

Eleanor and Franklin Roosevelt developed a strong relationship with administrators and students at Hunter College.

In 1940, while living in the townhouse on East 65th Street only three blocks from the campus, Eleanor began dropping in for informal visits with students in the office of *The Echo*, the college magazine. That was the beginning of numerous gatherings with students of the public liberal arts college founded in 1870 to train women to become teachers. Eleanor cheered on the basketball team and made public appearances on the campus where 350 full- and part-time faculty educated about 10,000 female students. She would make more than two dozen visits to Hunter over two decades and remain engaged with the college until the year before she died in 1962.[295]

At one of Eleanor's appearances in 1942, the president of the senior class, a girl from the Bronx named Bella Savitzky, sat on the stage. Three decades after her graduation in that year, now as Bella Abzug, she won a seat in the House of Representatives, serving from 1971 until 1977.[296]

Franklin Roosevelt had his own connection with Hunter. The Public Works Administration, one of FDR's New Deal programs, had funded construction of the college's North Building on Park Avenue. It replaced an 1873 Gothic-style structure destroyed in a fire on February 14, 1936. Mayor Fiorello LaGuardia had secured $6.5 million from the federal program to build a much larger replacement.[297]

FDR's one official visit to the campus was to see the recently completed North Building on October 28, 1940. The president came on stage, aided by his son James, along with dignitaries including the mayor, Hunter President George N. Shuster and New York Governor Herbert H. Lehman.[298] Former student Anna M. Trinsey later recalled the sound of "all 2,600 of us expressing our hearts' welcome" to the president. Freshman Marion Shomer Greene remembered "his appearance proved more moving than anyone anticipated, because we hadn't known how crippled he was....A lump rose in my throat at the sight of the effort our president had to make to walk just eight steps. I glanced around the audience, and many people had tears in their eyes....When he reached the podium, he stood by himself, holding onto the desk. We applauded him wildly, while he smiled the famous Roosevelt smile."[299]

The president's connection with the college strengthened four months after the double townhouse on East 65th Street was offered for sale following the death of Sara Roosevelt. Hunter President Shuster wrote to FDR on January 15, 1942, acting on an idea proposed by Dr. Abram L. Sachar, national director of the Hillel Foundation. Shuster asked if the president would be willing to sell the house to the college to become a center for religious and social groups.[300]

With the strong support of his wife, Franklin agreed not only to sell the townhouse to Hunter but also to cut the asking price by $10,000 to $50,000. Shuster suggested that the property be purchased by a nonprofit organization formed by Jewish, Protestant and Catholic religious groups and be open to all students. A committee formed to carry out the purchase was led by Joseph P. Day, a prominent figure in the city's real estate industry. Its honorary chairmen were Omaha, Nebraska banker Henry Monsky, president of the national B'nai B'rith Jewish organization; John S. Burke of the Altman Foundation and the B. Altman department store to represent the Catholic groups; and attorney Charles H. Tuttle, who had run against FDR for governor in 1930 and was a member of the board of the Greater New York Federation of Churches and of the Board of Higher Education, to represent Protestant groups. Aaron C. Horn, chairman of the executive committee of Sun Chemical Corporation, was named treasurer.

The president wrote to Monsky on March 19, 1942, saying, "I want to do all I can to help and because I am very certain that my mother would have been greatly interested in the Interfaith House, I want to have the privilege of subscribing $1,000 in my mother's name toward the total of the $50,000 fund. I do not think, of course, that this should be publicized but I have no objection if you want to tell some of your fellow trustees about it."[301] FDR wanted his $1,000 to be used to buy books to restock his former library.

After the committee raised the money to buy the house by June 1942, the sale was completed that summer. A bill was introduced in the state legislature to charter the Hunter College Student Social, Community and Religious Clubs Association in 1943 to "serve without discrimination the educational, spiritual, charitable and social needs of the students of Hunter College." Governor Thomas E. Dewey signed the bill on March 20, 1943.[302]

At the June 24, 1942 Hunter commencement, where Eleanor was the guest speaker, Aaron Horn announced that a committee of thirty-three citizens was donating the property to the college for use as a community house. Horn said the Sara Delano Roosevelt Interfaith House would be dedicated to "the ideal of religious freedom and the democratic way of living." In accepting the gift, Shuster said that 120 extracurricular organizations would be using the building and that it would help "prepare college girls in the best possible way for the 'new functions of leadership which will unquestionably be open to women when the war is over.'"[303]

The *New York Times* wrote that the townhouse would become "the first center of unity of its kind in New York City."[304]

To convert the building for its new use, the college hired the architectural firm of Shreve, Lamb & Harmon. The architects had previously designed the Empire State Building in 1931 and the college's new building at 695 Park Avenue. Their plan called for partially removing the walls between the dining and drawing rooms to create larger open spaces. The existing stoves were removed and added to a scrap metal drive conducted by the college to help the war effort.[305]

A Roosevelt House League, whose members included the college president's wife and the spouses of the chief fundraisers who purchased the house, was established to raise funds to purchase furnishings guided by volunteer decorators from Bloomingdale's and Altman's department stores. Hunter alumnae and others donated furniture, curtains, rugs and artwork. Besides contributing money, Franklin Roosevelt donated books and mementos to establish a library in No. 49 in memory of his mother. A portrait of her, a copy of a 1940 original at Hyde Park by artist Douglas Granville Chandor, was hung in that room. A second library established in No. 47 featured a portrait of the president by English painter Frank Salisbury that was a copy of the original at the New York Genealogical and Biological Society, of which FDR was a member.[306]

When the renovation was completed in November 1943, Hunter President Shuster told the *Alumnae News* that more than one thousand people from across the country had contributed to the fundraising effort. He noted that the project was the first of its kind in New York City in "promoting interfaith activity and fraternalism among the different religions."[307]

There were references to the ongoing war in Europe at the dedication ceremony held on November 22, 1943, in the college auditorium. FDR and other religious and political leaders were invited, but the president was en route to Tehran for an Allied summit with Winston Churchill and Joseph Stalin. He sent a message of support with Eleanor. Mayor LaGuardia was among the dignitaries at the event, which was broadcast live by the city's radio station, WNYC.[308]

After several musical performances, Shuster introduced the first lady to the crowd of 2,500 attendees. Eleanor read the message that her husband had written:

> *I feel that my dear mother would be very happy in the realization of plans whereby the old home in East Sixty-fifth Street, with all of its memories of joy and sorrow, is now to become Interfaith House, dedicated to mutual understanding and goodwill among students matriculating in Hunter College. It is to me of happy significance that this place of sacred memories is to become the first college center established for the high purpose of mutual understanding among Protestants, Jewish, and Catholic students. I hope this movement for toleration will grow and prosper until there is a similar establishment in every institution of higher learning in the land, the spirit of which shall be unity in essentials, liberty in non-essentials, and in all things charity. In that spirit we should all treasure in our hearts and souls the admonition of the grand Old Testament prophet* [in Micah 6:8], *"What does the Lord require of thee but to do justly, and to love mercy, and to walk humbly with thy God."*[309]

Eleanor described the family's history with the townhouse and her expectations for it in the future. "No houses have a better background for the use they will now serve," she stated. "Always in both houses, there was an effort to look on all human beings with respect, and to have a true understanding of the points of view of others."[310]

LaGuardia followed the first lady and spoke about how New York City had made real progress in promoting racial and religious harmony. He described Roosevelt House as a means for "conquering hatred, prejudice, and ignorance." Always quick with a joke, the mayor added that "there are only five or six people in the world I really dislike, and they all happen to be in Germany just now."[311]

Eleanor summarized her remarks about her mother-in-law and husband at the event in her November 24 syndicated newspaper column, "My Day": "We lived in one of these houses off and on for a number of years, but my mother-in-law lived in hers steadily for many years....She was very tolerant of all other religions. My husband is particularly glad that something, which he feels she would have approved, is going to be carried on in her house. I think she [Sara] would have been interested in having work go on in those houses which will bring about greater understanding and tolerance in young people."[312]

When Eleanor returned to New York City a week after the dedication, her itinerary included a stop at the Sara Delano Roosevelt Interfaith House. In her December 1 syndicated column, the first lady wrote, "It was interesting to go through it and to see how it had been adapted to its new uses. There have been very few structural changes, but those which have been made certainly increase its availability for its present purpose. There were girls in

Undated photograph of Eleanor Roosevelt with young women at Roosevelt House. *Roosevelt House Public Policy Institute, Hunter College, CUNY.*

all of the rooms, and I am sure that this is going to be a successful and useful experiment. The willingness of young people of different religious faiths to live and to work under the same roof is sure to bring about helpful discussion and better understanding among them."[313]

To "carry on the ideals and spirit of Sara Delano Roosevelt," as Eleanor put it, the college assigned a range of cultural and religious groups to be based in the building. The groups drew lots to determine their office space. The social and athletic organizations in No. 47 included the Pan-Hellenic Association, the Athletic Association, the Alumnae Association and eighteen sororities. It also had a game room. No. 49 was earmarked for religious groups. These included the Newman Club, a chapter of the organization that the Catholic Church operated at non-Catholic colleges. It was on the fourth floor, just below the Protestant groups and just above the headquarters of Hillel, the Jewish group. The Toussaint L'Ouverture Society for the Study of African-American History and Culture, founded in 1936, received an office at Roosevelt House as well. Dr. Margaret Rendt, who was appointed the first faculty house director, described Roosevelt House in 1960 as "a little U.N." Rendt worked with a council of representatives from the student groups to manage activities and schedules. Alumnae and neighborhood volunteers helped staff the reception desk during the evening. Hunter also hired a live-in custodian.[314]

With so many organizations meeting and working out of Roosevelt House, there could be five hundred students in the building on any given night. Many students made lasting relationships and partnerships, including marriage, there.

Gabriella Hoertrich Bender, class of 1948, loved to visit and browse the books in the library. In 1946, she was serving as a hostess for a social event when she met her future husband. Navy veteran Henry Bender, class of 1950, was one of the first men to attend Hunter's Bronx campus under the GI Bill of Rights. They were married two years later.[315] Joan Hansen Grabe, class of '60, said she was "courted" at Roosevelt House by her future husband and returned with him five decades later to mark their golden wedding anniversary.[316]

Irene Dwartz Lindenberg, a 1948 graduate, met her future husband at a house party for servicemen on Thanksgiving weekend 1945.

> *Since we didn't have enough men to go around at our little party we asked one of those, I think he was an Air Force man, to go down to the USO at*

Hunter College students meet under a portrait of Sara Delano Roosevelt at Roosevelt House. *Roosevelt House Public Policy Institute, Hunter College, CUNY.*

Temple Emanu-El which was right down the street. So he brought back a couple of guys and we had a very pleasant evening, dancing and we had refreshments. A couple of my friends decided they were going to go out afterwards and "would I join them?" and I said, "Well I'd love to, but I can't." Single girls didn't go anywhere in those days, you went only if you had an escort. I hadn't met anybody so this soldier came over to me and said "Irene, who would you like to go with? Find a guy and I'll ask him to take you." I looked around and I saw this young man standing there, a soldier, who was taller than I was and that was important, because I was 5'7" I said, "him." My friend went over and spoke to this soldier and said, "Would you like to go out with us" and he said, "Well I don't have a date" so he said "How about her?" He pointed to me and I watched through the corner of my eye as he gave me the up and down and he said, "Sure" so they brought him over and introduced us. That was it. We went to the Tavern on the Green that night and drank and danced and he was a wonderful dancer and that was the beginning of our friendship and marriage. So fate had him there that night.[317]

Some of the students held their weddings in Roosevelt House, taking advantage of a rental fee of only fifty dollars. One of them was 1947 graduate Elizabeth Thal Kahn. Her family had come to the United States in 1937 as refugees, and a decade later she was finishing college and engaged to a graduate student. The Hillel advisor suggested the venue for a modest wedding. "This was such a wonderful privilege for me since I always associated President Roosevelt with our escape from Germany and our well-being in this country," she said. "To be married under the portrait of Sara Delano Roosevelt who looked sternly upon us as if saying 'This is a serious manner' was awesome."[318]

The importance of Roosevelt House to the student body is evident in comments by Klara Silverstein, who wrote that "the social life at Hunter was through Roosevelt House, because Hillel and all the other religious organizations, as well as the social organizations, were there.…I got to know people of many different backgrounds in terms of religion and ethnicity and it all happened at Roosevelt House." Alumna Josie Levine, class of 1964, recalled that "my girlfriends, who were other ethnicities, dragged me off to their meetings, and I dragged them off to mine. The fact that Mrs. Roosevelt had lived there, that the president had lived there—that this was a house where they had thought these wonderful thoughts, and planned careers—to me that was like touching history, and having history touch me."[319]

A May 31, 1992 wedding was probably the last event at Roosevelt House before it was closed because of deterioration. Larry Shore, a member of the Hunter Film & Media Studies Department, married Sarah Sills Ragan that day.[320]

From the beginning, part of the Roosevelt House mission was improving interracial understanding. This reflected the heritage of Hunter, which began admitting Black students in 1873, three years after it opened, making it one of the early colleges in America to do that. Helene H. Goldfarb, a 1951 graduate, recounted that "I was a member of an inter-racial nonsectarian sorority which was the only one of its kind at Hunter and we spent many, many long wonderful hours and days at Roosevelt House just working in… our little office and it was very important to us to know that this was the place where the president and his wife had lived. I was there maybe every other day during the four years I was at Hunter. I remember walking with my friend Ruby Saunders, who was Black, down Park Avenue and having

Undated early photograph of women of color meeting at Roosevelt House. *Roosevelt House photo.*

everyone look at us, because that was unusual, and yet going into Hunter and going into Roosevelt House none of that meant anything to us."[321]

At Hunter, "House Plans," clubs founded by students with similar interests, were the primary organizers of social activity, including parties, wartime military receptions and dances. The House Plans were akin to sororities, but they were not affiliated with national associations and their membership fees were very affordable. Lucille Freedberg, class of 1944, remembered that "the dues may have been 50 cents or a dollar or something like that. And certainly everybody was eligible, nobody had to worry about getting in, everybody was accepted."[322]

Another House Plan member, 1949 graduate Joan Swift Hollander, said the building was special as a "place for socializing, because we were a commuter college and we all after class took the subway home, but this was a place to go to after school, evenings, weekends and have a social life connected with our college." Patricia Creamer Mulligan, class of 1953, recalled, "I had a wonderful House Plan, Maxwell '53 and we all encouraged each other and we all learned from each other. And we had wonderful parties and mother-daughter teas and wonderful meetings." [323]

"It was a wonderful social gathering place," said 1962 graduate and future Eleanor Roosevelt biographer Blanche Wiesen Cook. "Folks got married there. I had book parties there long after I graduated. It really was a splendid social forum sort of place....The student council had great events there, the National Student Association had meetings there, all the religious clubs had meetings there, and it was great center of extracurricular activities."[324]

For students from a lower economic strata, seeing Roosevelt House gave them a glimpse of how more wealthy New Yorkers lived. Irene Swartz, class of '46, recalled that the house seemed "very elegant, much more so than probably a lot of the homes we came from." Nancy Vochis Gabriel, class of '43, said "it was very elegant surroundings. It didn't have the institutional feel of the college. I was suddenly surrounded by these lovely portraits and lovely furniture, and remember, all of us came from primarily middle-class and lower middle-class families."[325]

Since Roosevelt House was created during World War II, the conflict was reflected in events in the building. During the war, there were weekly dances modeled after the Hollywood Canteen and open to members of the armed forces who were in the city. Ruth Goodman Cohen, class of '46, said, "It is considered our patriotic duty to attend the Roosevelt House canteen to try to build up the morale of those fellows. Those battle-bound young men were able to forget briefly what lay ahead, by chatting and relaxing in the pleasant surroundings of Roosevelt House's upstairs salon" in the former drawing rooms. "The house represented for me a bright spot in a terrifying world of depressing events."[326] During the war, one House Plan was named "Norris, '46" in honor of a Hunter faculty member who was serving in the South Pacific.[327]

The "depressing events" marked at the townhouse included FDR's death on April 12, 1945. Hunter students remembered him for his connection to the house and as the only president many of them had ever known. After he died in Georgia, students brought flowers to Roosevelt House in his memory. And the Roosevelt House League published a memorial notice in the *New York Times* on April 15: "Writing from the New York home where he once lived, we bow in profound sorrow to the decree of Providence which took from the nation its great President, Franklin Delano Roosevelt."[328]

Besides serving Hunter students, the house occasionally hosted special events for the public. On the tenth anniversary of its opening in 1953, the

A World War II dance at Roosevelt House. *Roosevelt House Public Policy Institute, Hunter College, CUNY.*

Association of Neighbors and Friends of Roosevelt House sponsored a program on the "Dutch Founders of Our City" with an exhibit of eighty-four Dutch paintings and etchings to mark the anniversary of the house, the three hundredth anniversary of New York's incorporation as a city and the Roosevelt family's roots in the Netherlands.[329]

The house also gained some fame in 1960 when scenes for the movie *Sunrise at Campobello* starring Ralph Bellamy as FDR and Greer Garson as Eleanor were filmed inside the building. The movie was based on the 1958 play by Dore Schary that covers FDR's life from when he contracted polio in 1921 to his political comeback at the Democratic convention of 1924.[330]

Eleanor Roosevelt continued to be a frequent presence at Roosevelt House. Lucille Friedberg, a 1944 graduate, recalled watching the first lady on the first floor from the second level and being impressed by how tall she was. "But she seemed so huge to me because of her brain as well as her stature," she added. Carolyn Nussbaum Lynch, class of '54, noted that Roosevelts were so involved with the college that the students felt like part of their family. Eleanor took a personal interest in many of those students. Rita Abrams, class of '54, met Eleanor at Hunter and began working as one of her assistants. When her father resisted Rita's desire to attend law school,

Eleanor wrote a letter in support of her plan. Rita graduated from Harvard Law School, had a groundbreaking career at the United Nations and then played a key role in the rehabilitation of Roosevelt House.[331]

Blanche Wiesen Cook, the 1962 graduate who was president of the student government before going on to graduate school, became a professor at John Jay College and the Graduate Center of City University of New York. Cook, who published the three-volume biography *Eleanor Roosevelt* between 1992 and 2016, remembered the "tall and majestic" former first lady visiting Roosevelt House late in life before her death on November 7, 1962. When Eleanor arrived, "the energy in the room transformed. It was electric and she gave a very heartening and galvanizing speech." It was early in the civil rights movement, and Eleanor urged the students to "go south for freedom." Cook said, "I think she really inspired many of us to think about our role for the future."[332]

Because of its special place in political and city history, Roosevelt House was designated a landmark by the New York City Landmarks Preservation Commission on September 25, 1973.[333] And on March 28, 1980, it was listed on the National Register of Historic Places.[334] But those designations would not be enough to save the building from deterioration, closure and the threat of demolition.

13
ELEANOR ROOSEVELT ON HER OWN

When FDR placed the East 65th Street townhouse on the market in 1942 after the death of his mother, Franklin and Eleanor signed a four-year lease for a seven-room apartment at 29 Washington Square West, and Eleanor moved the family's New York City possessions there. After FDR's death in Warm Springs in April 1945, Eleanor continued to live on Washington Square.[335]

The Greenwich Village apartment was Eleanor's home in 1946 when President Harry S. Truman appointed her as a delegate to the United Nations General Assembly. In that position, which she held until 1952, Eleanor served as the first chairperson of the Commission on Human Rights and played an instrumental role in drafting the Universal Declaration of Human Rights.[336]

By the end of 1949, she was renting a suite in the Park Sheraton Hotel at 202 West 56th Street, where she enjoyed views of Central Park. After four years there, Eleanor decided she wanted her own home. So in 1953, she leased an apartment at 211 East 62nd Street. Eleanor wrote about the move in her "My Day" column on August 31, 1953. "Everything in my New York apartment is more or less upside down, for the packers are coming on Monday to move my belongings to my new little apartment on East 62nd Street," she said. "I have been in the Park Sheraton Hotel so long that I hated to tear myself away, but I think it will be better to have a little place where I can keep house and have my dogs in New York with me. I have a little garden, which should make a pleasant difference, and being over on

Eleanor Roosevelt in November 1949 holding a copy of the Declaration of Human Rights that she helped draft as a United States delegate to the United Nations at the UN's temporary headquarters in the old gymnasium at what was then Hunter College's Bronx campus and is now Lehman College. *UN photo.*

the East Side will make it easier to get to my AAUN [American Association for the United Nations] office in the Carnegie Endowment Building on East 46th Street, opposite the U.N."[337]

The AAUN was formed during World War II to promote support in the United States for creation of the United Nations. After Eleanor Roosevelt completed her term in 1952 as a U.S. representative to the United Nations General Assembly, she walked into the association's New York office and volunteered the next year. The office, which was then located at 45 East 65th Street, was conveniently located next to her former home.

She began a campaign to increase support for the UN through personal appearances and fundraising efforts. The former first lady helped create AAUN chapters on college campuses and in communities across the country.[338]

Eleanor decorated the East 62nd Street space with a table whose base was a carved wooden elephant and four watercolors by her confidant and political advisor Louis Howe. When her lease expired in 1958, Eleanor moved back to the Park Sheraton Hotel.[339]

Eleanor's final residence in the city was suggested by her friend Edna Gurewitsch, a successful art dealer who was the wife of her personal physician, David Gurewitsch. Edna's idea was that Eleanor might want to share a townhouse with her and her husband. When Eleanor liked the concept, Edna searched the city for a property that would accommodate the three of them as well as her husband's practice. She selected a townhouse at 55 East 74th Street. It was one of a group of eight similar buildings designed in 1889 by the architectural partnership of Buchman and Deisler. The neo-Renaissance building was fronted by Greek columns with a sweeping curved staircase leading to the upper floors from the main entrance area's marble floor.[340]

The bedroom of Eleanor Roosevelt's last apartment on East 74th Street. *Courtesy of the Franklin D. Roosevelt Library.*

Eleanor wrote about the townhouse in her "My Day" column on December 2, 1959, saying she would

> *have a real housewarming soon, and will ask as many of my friends as possible. Many of them are interested, I know, in what I hope is my last move in New York City.*
>
> *Dr. David Gurewitsch and I bought this house together, and he and his wife are comfortably settled on the upper floors. Someday I also will have the floor below the one I now occupy and then I will be extremely comfortable. But even now I am quite content, if still a little crowded.*
>
> *It is nice to be out of a hotel and in my own home again, though everyone in the Park-Sheraton Hotel was so kind and considerate that I feel I owe them a debt of gratitude for making the past year as comfortable for me in the city as it could be made.*[341]

Eventually, Eleanor occupied the first three floors of the townhouse while writing for *McCall's* magazine, turning out her "My Day" column and using it as base for her extensive lecturing. The Gurewitsches were on the fourth and fifth floors. Eleanor died in her bed at the townhouse on November 7, 1962. Over the years, the townhouse, which still exists, has had many subsequent owners.[342]

14
THE RESTORATION OF ROOSEVELT HOUSE

After a half century of heavy use by Hunter College students, Sara Delano Roosevelt Memorial House had deteriorated considerably. The roof had begun to leak, and the stairways were no longer safe to use. With temporary repairs no longer sufficient, the college closed the building in 1992. The headline in the *Hunter Envoy* student newspaper read: "Another One Bites the Dust."[343]

The empty building was the site of a decorator showcase in 1994, but by 1997 architectural historian Christopher Gray described it as a "bedraggled town house…with its rotting window frames, stained brick and neglected iron doors."[344]

Roosevelt House might have remained closed or even been sold if not for Jennifer J. Raab. Almost a decade after the doors were shut, Raab was hired as Hunter's president. When she arrived on campus in 2001, Raab declared: "It's a moral obligation to make this house flourish again."[345]

At the time, the entire City University of New York system was in financial peril and its academic standing had slipped, so few considered Roosevelt House a priority. Selling the property was suggested to generate needed revenue. Raab, however, viewed Roosevelt House as representing Hunter at its best and most ambitious and well worth preserving and reusing.[346]

And Raab had the perfect background for getting it done. Before coming to Hunter, for seven years, "I was the landmarks commissioner for New York City, so I became aware that there was a home of one of the most important presidents and first ladies when they lived in New York City, and it was completely shuttered," Raab said in an interview with the author after she retired in 2023. "And we had a grant program at landmarks for renovation, so we gave a small grant to Hunter and I learned more about the house. And when I became president a year or two later, I really approached this as a strategic vision for the college."[347]

While the initial matching grant paid for cleaning and repairing the façade in 2002, Raab understood that fully saving and reusing the townhouse would be a huge challenge. "This is an incredibly important historic home, but it was in really completely unusable condition at that time," she related. "The water had been pouring through the roof, the stairs were not safe to walk on. And while there had been attempts over the years to restore it, none of them had been successful."

Her effort to save the building came at a critical time. "It was a turning point for the college," Raab said. "Open admissions had ended and there was a lot of disinvestment in the system. And I really thought strategically if we could restore this home to its historic status and bring the legacy of the Roosevelts to a great public college and infuse that vision of social action, of using government to make people's lives better, which is really what they stood for, and to really be a positive force within government, that would be great message to our students," who are mostly children of immigrant parents. She also envisioned the structure as being "a gathering and rallying point for the faculty. So I really pushed for that idea to risk to restore it."

Raab knew that others at the college thought there were much higher priority items to deal with before worrying about the Roosevelt home. "It was obvious at that point that there were so many needs in the school and it was not necessarily obvious to…spend resources to reopen it. But I thought that would really be a transformation."

To move forward with the project, Raab continued,

> *We needed to make the case to the governor, George Pataki, who was very strong preservationist, and to the* [City University of New York] *chancellor, and they said there are many competing needs. But this seemed to be more than just physical property. It was what it could do for the college. And it was something for the students so that they could engage in public policy and human rights study, internships, civic engagement, bring together the very large faculty at Hunter that did policy work, so you could give them a place to gather and to do their research and to connect with each other. And then there's also our role as a public institution, and they felt strongly about that we were a neighbor in the city. And we also as a public institution*

> *should be opening our doors more to the neighborhood for them to engage in intellectual conversation. But it was not an obvious decision. It proved to be a wonderful restoration and all those things followed.*

Once Raab had convinced the governor and other key players that the building was worth saving, she arranged for ownership to be transferred from the Hunter College Foundation to the City University so that the college could use public funding for the renovation.[348]

Then the school hired the architectural firm of James Polshek Partners. It had an impressive track record, having designed the Clinton Presidential Library in Arkansas and the Rose Center at the American Museum of Natural History. Polshek partner Richard Olcott was designated the project architect. Meanwhile, Raab raised $24 million in city and private funding for the restoration.[349]

"One of the wonderful things that happened in this whole project was really having architects who helped to translate your vision into physical structure," Raab said. "We really wanted it to be this gathering place for students, faculty and community and be something very special with incredible history that would really bring people in to focus on the problems of today in a place that was very special for what had happened in the past. But it didn't have any place that you could have a program. So it took the Polshek firm to come up with this idea of really blowing out the backyard and excavating it and creating the beautiful auditorium where we could have gatherings and programming and then break into lunch or receptions or breakout rooms."

The architects' ambitious concept was combining two lower levels—the old kitchens and cellar—and the space under the backyard to create an auditorium. By 2005, the architectural plans were finalized.[350]

To make the vision a reality, Rabb said, "I had to get down to the landmark commission to get approval, and that was sort of fun to go back down to my old agency. It was a very wonderful surprise that we could physically change a historic building within the parameters of the landmark rules to function for modern needs. But everything was done according to the rules and it was very successful."

One of those rules required an unusual construction technique. "The backyard had to be excavated by using wheelbarrows because backhoes were banned from city townhouses," Rabb explained.

Construction began in 2006 and was completed in four years. The auditorium, which seats one hundred, features the words of Franklin

Roosevelt's "Four Freedoms" speech on the rear wall.[351] Upstairs, former maids' rooms were converted to scholars' suites for visiting faculty and lecturers. The dining rooms and parlors became classrooms and exhibition and meeting spaces. The second-floor library on Sara's side remained a library for students and is also used for seminars. FDR's library remains a library and meeting place for distinguished guests. A new elevator provides access to all the floors. Raab ensured that original architectural details were preserved. Portraits that had been on display in the house since 1943 were conserved and returned to the walls along with other artworks added to the collection.[352]

Raab relied on two important advisors during the restoration: Curtis Roosevelt and William vanden Heuvel. Roosevelt, who had been born in the townhouse in 1930 and lived there in his childhood, was FDR and Eleanor's oldest surviving grandchild. He worked at the United Nations for eighteen years as an international civil servant, and he helped save and restore Eleanor Roosevelt's home at Val-Kill near Hyde Park. Raab recalled that "Curtis was also passionately committed to making sure that Roosevelt House was also renovated and restored and reopened. And he worked for that for a long time before I arrived at Hunter. And when we did get to meet, he walked right into my office and sat down, barely said hello and said, 'You've got to get this house renovated.'"

Vanden Heuvel had been devoted to the Roosevelts since he was a teenager and hitchhiked to Hyde Park to attend FDR's funeral. He was a lawyer who served in the administration of President John F. Kennedy, was U.S. ambassador to the European office of the United Nations in Geneva (1977–79) and deputy ambassador to the United Nations (1979–1981) during the administration of President Jimmy Carter. He supported several Roosevelt institutions and was the driving force in raising funds to build FDR Four Freedoms State Park on Roosevelt Island. "He advised me on the future of a renewed Roosevelt House as a public policy center," Raab said. "He always believed that we could create a place to teach and inspire the next generation of civic leaders to follow the Roosevelts, and so we have."[353]

On November 15, 2010, United Nations Secretary-General Ban Ki-moon cut a ribbon to rededicate Roosevelt House. He commented that "FDR's friend and contemporary, Winston Churchill, once said: 'We shape our dwellings, and afterwards our dwellings shape us.' If that is true, then surely 49 East 65th street is one of the most important houses of the modern era. These brick and limestone walls witnessed the birth of two legacies that

Hunter College President Jennifer Raab with the Dalai Lama at Roosevelt House in 2010. *Roosevelt House Public Policy Institute, Hunter College, CUNY.*

have shaped our world: …a new era of multilateral cooperation for international peace, security and social welfare and an explicit commitment by all nations to recognize fundamental freedoms and universal human rights, including equal rights for men and women."

In keeping with Raab's vision for reimagining use of the structure, the building became a public policy institute educating students on policy and human rights, issues important to the original occupants, and hosting a variety of public programs. Guests have included the Dalai Lama; President Bill Clinton; former Secretary of State Hillary Clinton; House Speaker Nancy Pelosi and other members of Congress; and historian-authors, including Robert Caro and Doris Kearns Goodwin, author of *No Ordinary Time*, a biography of Franklin and Eleanor Roosevelt.[354]

"I thought that it would really be a transformation and it did turn out to be that, to be a symbol of how we restored Hunter from being a really storied institution that seemed to have been disinvested over the years to a premier public college in New York City," Raab said. "So Roosevelt House really became a symbol of what we did at Hunter as well as restoring the house itself."

Today, Roosevelt House continues to prepare Hunter students to become the next generation of informed global citizens. Two undergraduate programs offer courses in public policy and human rights. Civic dialogue is promoted by book talks, conferences and special events. Students and the public are engaged through exhibits, film screenings and tours.

And Roosevelt House is again the only original home of an American president in New York City that maintains its historic integrity and is open to the public.

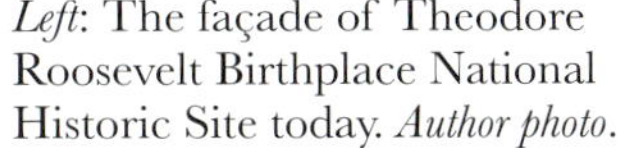

Left: The façade of Theodore Roosevelt Birthplace National Historic Site today. *Author photo*.

Right: The stairway at Theodore Roosevelt Birthplace. *Author photo*.

Above: The parlor at Theodore Roosevelt Birthplace today. *Author photo*.

Left: The dining room at Theodore Roosevelt Birthplace today. The pieces of furniture are among the oldest in the house, dating to the early 1800s. The set was previously used by TR's grandfather Cornelius Van Schaack Roosevelt in his home on Union Square. *Author photo*.

Right: One piece of original Roosevelt family china on display in the dining room at Theodore Roosevelt Birthplace. *Author photo*.

Below: The master bedroom at Theodore Roosevelt Birthplace. The bedroom set was reportedly purchased by Theodore and Mittie Roosevelt about 1870 at a cost of $3,500. It was the most extravagant purchase made for the home on East 20th Street. Although the rosewood elements could be sourced in the United States, the satinwood came from the Far East. *Author photo*.

The nursery at Theodore Roosevelt Birthplace. *Author photo.*

Crib used by Theodore Roosevelt on display in the nursery at Theodore Roosevelt Birthplace National Historic Site. *Author photo.*

Left: A child's rocking chair original to the house at Theodore Roosevelt Birthplace. *Author photo*.

Right: Otis elevator equipment from 1920 in the basement of Theodore Roosevelt Birthplace. *Author photo*.

Left: Theodore Roosevelt's Rough Rider uniform on display at Theodore Roosevelt Birthplace. *Author photo*.

Right: The shirt Theodore Roosevelt was wearing when he was shot and almost killed by a would-be assassin in Milwaukee on October 14, 1912, during his presidential campaign as the Progressive Party candidate, on display at Theodore Roosevelt Birthplace. Note the bullet hole near his heart. *Author photo*.

Above: The case for Theodore Roosevelt's eyeglasses with a bullet hole in the lower right corner from the assassination attempt in Milwaukee during the 1912 presidential campaign on display at Theodore Roosevelt Birthplace. The bullet passed through the case and his folded speech, slowing it enough to save TR's life. He characteristically and famously insisted on giving his entire speech before receiving medical attention. *Author photo.*

Left: A bronze sculpture of Theodore Roosevelt as he looked during a famous 1903 camping trip to Yosemite with naturalist John Muir in the Theodore Roosevelt Rotunda at the American Museum of Natural History. *Author photo.*

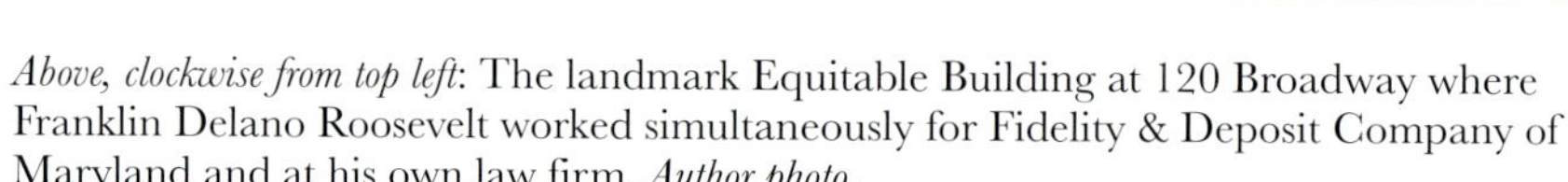

Above, clockwise from top left: The landmark Equitable Building at 120 Broadway where Franklin Delano Roosevelt worked simultaneously for Fidelity & Deposit Company of Maryland and at his own law firm. *Author photo.*

The twin townhouse that Sara Delano Roosevelt had built for herself and Franklin and Eleanor Roosevelt and their children at 47 and 49 East 65th Street. They moved in in 1908. The building is now Roosevelt House, owned by Hunter College. *Author photo.*

Family crest on the façade of East 65th Street townhouse. *Author photo.*

The exterior of Eleanor Roosevelt's final residence at 55 East 74th Street. *Author photo*.

The east stairway hall of Roosevelt House before the 2006 restoration by James Polshek Partners. *Ennead Architects*.

Roosevelt House during restoration. *Ennead Architects*.

Right: Entrance to Roosevelt House today. *Author photo*.

Left: The Roosevelt House entrance hall today. *Author photo*.

Left: Roosevelt House staircase today. *Author photo*.

Right: The original elevator on Sara Delano Roosevelt's side of Roosevelt House today. *Author photo*.

Sara Delano Roosevelt's library in Roosevelt House where FDR's portrait has hung since 1943. *Author photo*.

FDR's library at Roosevelt House. *Author photo*.

Opposite, top: An original fireplace at Roosevelt House. *Author photo*.

Opposite, bottom: Auditorium at Roosevelt House. *Author photo*.

Above: Rear of auditorium at Roosevelt House with words from FDR's Four Freedoms section of his 1941 State of the Union Address. *Author photo*.

Right: United Nations Secretary-General Ban Ki-moon speaking at the dedication of Roosevelt House Public Policy Institute on November 15, 2010. *Roosevelt House Public Policy Institute, Hunter College, CUNY*.

Clockwise from top left: Hunter College President Jennifer Raab with the Dalai Lama at Roosevelt House in 2010. *Roosevelt House Public Policy Institute, Hunter College, CUNY.*

Hunter College President Jennifer Raab with Arthur Browne and his family with the image he shot as a New York Daily News photographer that captured FDR with his leg braces showing when the president visited East 65th Street in September 1933. The Daily News never ran the photograph because of American newspapers' self-censorship policy of never showing Roosevelt's disability. *Roosevelt House Public Policy Institute, Hunter College, CUNY.*

Eleanor Roosevelt Memorial statue in Riverside Park. *Author photo.*

Appendix A

ROOSEVELT-RELATED SITES IN NEW YORK CITY

While the American Museum of Natural History, Theodore Roosevelt Birthplace and Roosevelt House at Hunter College are the main sites of interest for those curious about the family's connections to New York City, there are numerous other locations with Roosevelt ties. They are listed chronologically. All are in Manhattan unless otherwise noted.

Former location of Roosevelt & Son business, 94 Maiden Lane

This was the site of the Roosevelts' hardware business that later focused on selling imported plate glass before shifting solely to banking. The family sold its glass importing operation to a British firm in 1876 and moved its banking and investment business to new offices on Pine Street.[355]

Location of Cornelius Van Schaack Roosevelt home, Union Square

President Theodore Roosevelt's grandfather built a stately home on the southwest corner of Broadway and 14th Street in the 1830s after moving uptown from Maiden Lane, where the family hardware and plate glass importing business was located.

just salad
just salad
NYC Convenience
Retail For Lease

Opposite, clockwise from top left:

94 Maiden Lane today. *Author photo*.

The reconstructed and altered home of Robert B. Roosevelt today. *Author photo*.

LaGrange Terrace on Lafayette Street in Greenwich Village today. *Author photo*.

Right: Former location of home of Cornelius Van Schaack Roosevelt on Union Square at the southwest corner of Broadway and 14th Street. *Author photo*.

Warren Delano Jr. home, Colonnade Row/LaGrange Terrace, 428–434 Lafayette Street

Warren Delano Jr., an ancestor of Franklin Delano Roosevelt's mother, Sara, greatly boosted the family fortune through the opium trade. That allowed him to purchase large homes along the Hudson River and an elaborate townhouse at LaGrange Terrace on Lafayette Street next to his younger brother Franklin Hughes Delano. The Greek Revival building originally contained nine interconnected townhouses built between 1830 and 1832. Each was twenty-seven feet wide with twenty-six rooms. Today, only four of the townhouses remain in what is now called Colonnade Row: numbers 428, 430, 432 and 434. All are New York City landmarks also listed on the National Register of Historic Places.[356]

Plaque on the façade of Theodore Roosevelt Birthplace National Historic Site. *Author photo.*

Reconstructed Robert Barnwell Roosevelt home, 26 East 20th Street

This is the site of the brownstone home of Robert Barnwell Roosevelt, uncle of future president Theodore Roosevelt. RBR's father, Cornelius Van Schaack Roosevelt, provided twin adjacent brownstones for sons Robert and Theodore Sr. after they married. Robert married his first wife, Elizabeth Ellis Roosevelt, in 1850. After TR's death in 1919, the demolished structures were rebuilt by 1923 by the Woman's Roosevelt Memorial Association. The façade of RBR's house was changed to remove the stairs, entrance and other features to use the space for displays and a library for the re-created birthplace next door. See chapter 4 for more details.

Theodore Roosevelt Birthplace National Historic Site, 28 East 20th Street

The twenty-sixth president was born at this location between Park Avenue South and Broadway on October 27, 1858. The house where Theodore Roosevelt Sr. and Martha "Mittie" Bulloch Roosevelt raised their four children after their 1853 marriage was a wedding present from his father. The home where TR lived until age fourteen was demolished in 1916. After Roosevelt's death in 1919, the site was purchased by the Woman's Roosevelt Memorial Association and replicated by architect Theodate Pope Riddle. It opened in 1923 with furnishings donated by the family. The property was

6 West 57th Street today. *Author photo.*

donated to the park service in 1962. See chapters 2 and 3 of this book for more details.

Theodore Sr. and Mittie Roosevelt homesite, 6 West 57th Street

Theodore Sr. moved his family uptown to a newly built home (no longer extant) he had built in 1873 when he and his wife Mittie decided the 5th Avenue neighborhood around their home on East 20th Street had become too commercialized. The property was vacant and awaiting redevelopment in early 2025. See chapter 5 for more details.

West 45th Street

After their marriage, Theodore and Alice Roosevelt, probably in late 1882, moved into a house on West 45th Street next door to his sister Corinne and her husband, Douglas Robinson, while TR served in the state assembly. It is unclear whether they rented or bought the house. They moved back into the family's West 57th Street house when Alice became pregnant in 1883.

Calvary Episcopal Church, 277 Park Avenue South

This church at 21st Street was designed by James Renwick Jr., the architect who also designed St. Patrick's Cathedral, and it was completed in 1848. Many Roosevelts attended the church, and Elliott Roosevelt and Anna

Top: Calvary Episcopal Church today. *Author photo.*

Bottom left: Homesite of Anna "Bamie" Roosevelt at 422 Madison Avenue today. *Author photo.*

Bottom right: Eleanor Roosevelt birth site today. *Author photo.*

Clockwise from top left: Homesite of Bamie Roosevelt at 689 Madison Avenue from 1886 to 1893 as it appears today. *Author photo.*

56 West 37th Street today. *Author photo.*

Anna Hall Roosevelt home site today. *Author photo.*

Site of Ludlow Hall today. *Author photo.*

Rebecca Hall were married here on December 1, 1883. Their daughter Eleanor Roosevelt was baptized here in 1885.

Homesite of Anna "Bamie" Roosevelt, 422 Madison Avenue

Three months after her mother, Mittie, died in 1884, her oldest child, Anna, nicknamed Bamie, purchased a new brownstone (no longer extant) at this address between 48th and 49th Streets. While her brother Theodore was ranching in the Dakotas after the death of his wife Alice on the same day as his mother, Bamie raised her niece, also named Alice, until TR returned to New York for good in 1886. See chapter 6 for more details.

Eleanor Roosevelt birth site, 29 East 38th Street

This address between Madison and Park Avenues was the site of the brownstone home of Elliott and Anna Hall Roosevelt where Eleanor was born on October 11, 1884. See chapter 9 for more details.

Homesite of Bamie Roosevelt, 689 Madison Avenue

In 1886, TR's older sister spent $50,000 from her share of the sale proceeds from the family's West 57th Street house on a new home near 62nd Street. She lived there until moving to England in 1893. See chapter 6.

Elliott and Anna Roosevelt homesite, 56 West 37th Street

Elliott and Anna Roosevelt with Eleanor and their other children lived here after returning from Europe in 1887. See chapter 6 for more details.

Anna Hall Roosevelt homesite, 54 East 61st Street

Eleanor lived from age seven to ten in a house here bought by her mother while her father was in exile trying to deal with his alcoholism. The building is gone, as is its address, replaced by a large apartment building on the corner of 3rd Avenue.

Homesite of Eleanor's grandmother, Ludlow Hall, 11 West 37th Street

After the death of her mother in 1892, Eleanor lived with maternal grandmother Mary Livingston at Ludlow Hall, since demolished, west of 5th Avenue.

The Roosevelt Building, 841 Broadway

This eight-story Romanesque Revival/Renaissance Revival–style store and loft building between 13th and 14th Streets was designed by Stephen D. Hatch. It was built in 1894 for James A. Roosevelt and Robert Barnwell Roosevelt, uncles of future president Theodore Roosevelt. It housed garment manufacturers, including Carhart & Company, and the Biograph Company, one of the first American film studios.[357]

Elliott Roosevelt home, 313 West 102nd Street

Forced to stay away from his family, Eleanor's alcoholic father, Elliott Roosevelt, leased a townhouse at this address east of Riverside Drive before moving to Abingdon, Virginia, where he died on August 14, 1894, after a suicide attempt.

Ludlow-Parish House, 6–8 East 76th Street

The double townhouse that was located east of 5th Avenue was the home of Eleanor's cousin Susan Ludlow Parish and banker Henry Parish. Eleanor lived at No. 8 after she returned from school in Europe in 1902 when she turned eighteen until her marriage here on March 17, 1905.

Site of Rivington Street Settlement House, 95 Rivington Street

The building once located between Ludlow and Orchard Streets on the Lower East Side was where Eleanor taught classes to young girls twice a week after her coming out as a debutante in the winter of 1902–3.

Above: The Roosevelt Building today. *Author photo.*

Left: Elliott Roosevelt lived at 313 West 102nd Street east of Riverside Drive when he was forced to stay away from his family because of his alcoholism until his death on August 14, 1894. *Author photo.*

Opposite, top: Ludlow-Parish House. *Author photo.*

Opposite, bottom left: Site of Rivington Street Settlement House today. *Author photo.*

Opposite, bottom right: Church of the Incarnation today. *Author photo.*

Church of the Incarnation, 209 Madison Avenue

Eleanor attended this Episcopal church at 35th Street from 1902 into adulthood.

Columbia University, Broadway and 116th Street

Franklin Roosevelt attended Columbia Law School on the Morningside Heights campus from 1904 to 1907. The law school was located in Low Memorial Library from 1897 to 1910.

Sara Delano Roosevelt residence, 200 Madison Avenue

The site of the home between 35th and 36th Streets where FDR's mother lived while he attended Columbia Law School. The structure was replaced in 1926 by a twenty-five-story office building.

Webster Hotel, 40 West 45th Street

Newly married Franklin and Eleanor lived in an apartment at the Classical Revival–style hotel between 5th and 6th Avenues from March to June 1905 while he attended Columbia Law School. Built in 1902, it was added to the National Register of Historic Places in 1984. It functions today as The Midtown Executive Club and the Club Quarters Times Square–Midtown hotel.[358]

Draper House, 125 East 36th Street

The still-standing Italianate brownstone built around 1856 between Park and Lexington Avenues in the Murray Hill neighborhood was rented by Sara Delano Roosevelt for Eleanor and Franklin, at their request, in 1905. Sara furnished the house, which was near her own residence, and hired three servants. The couple rented it until 1908. Their two oldest children were born here: Anna in 1906 and James in 1907.

Carter, Ledyard and Milburn law office, 54 Wall Street

After Franklin Roosevelt passed the bar exam in the spring of 1907, he was hired as what he described as a "full-fledged office boy" or law clerk by the firm of Carter, Ledyard and Milburn. He worked there until 1910. The building was replaced in 1987 by a forty-seven-story office tower.

Roosevelt House, 47–49 East 65th Street

On Christmas Day 1906, Sara Delano Roosevelt presented her son, Franklin, and daughter-in-law, Eleanor, with a rough drawing depicting a double townhouse where she would live on one side and Franklin and Eleanor and their children on the other. Sara purchased a pair of four-story brownstones at 47 and 49 East 65th Street between Park and Madison Avenues and replaced them with the connected double townhouse. The Roosevelts moved in 1908 with Sara living in No. 47 while Franklin, Eleanor and their children Anna and James were in No. 49. FDR and his family lived on East 65th Street until they moved into the White House in 1933. Subsequently, they stayed at the house during visits to New York City. Sara continued to live in the townhouse when not at Hyde Park until her death in 1941. Franklin sold the house to Hunter College the following year. For more details, see chapters 10, 11, 12 and 14.

Franklin Delano Roosevelt law office, 52 Wall Street

From 1920 to 1924, FDR was a partner in the law firm of Emmet, Marvin & Roosevelt, located in a building at this address that was demolished in 1986. He could no longer work in the office after he contracted polio in 1921 because he was unable to climb the entrance stairs. But Roosevelt continued to be a partner in the firm for three more years, even after being hired in 1921 as a vice president and manager of the New York office of the Fidelity & Deposit Company of Maryland, which was located in the nearby Equitable Building at 120 Broadway.[359]

Equitable Building, 120 Broadway

In 1921, Franklin Roosevelt was hired as a vice president and manager of the New York office of the Fidelity & Deposit Company of Maryland located at this prestigious downtown edifice erected in 1915 between Pine and Cedar streets. The forty-four-floor structure was the largest office building in the world at that time, with more than one million square feet of space.

While working at Fidelity, FDR managed to also be a partner in two law firms. The first was Emmet, Marvin & Roosevelt, as noted in the previous listing. His second law firm was Roosevelt & O'Connor, which operated from 1925 to 1928 from a different floor than Fidelity at 120 Broadway. The firm existed until Roosevelt's inauguration as president in 1933.

Top: Columbia Law School library about 1904 when it was housed in Low Library on Columbia University's campus. *University Archives, Rare Book & Manuscript Library, Columbia University Libraries.*

Bottom left: The former Webster Hotel today. *Author photo.*

Bottom right: Draper House today. *Author photo.*

Clockwise from top left: Former site of Carter, Ledyard and Milburn law office. *Author photo.*

The twin townhouse that Sara Delano Roosevelt had built for herself and Franklin and Eleanor Roosevelt and their children at 47 and 49 East 65th Street. They moved in in 1908. The building is now Roosevelt House, owned by Hunter College. *Author photo.*

The landmark Equitable Building at 120 Broadway where Franklin Delano Roosevelt worked simultaneously for Fidelity & Deposit Company of Maryland and at his own law firm. *Author photo.*

Former site of Franklin Delano Roosevelt's Wall Street law office from 1920 to 1924. *Author photo.*

Clockwise from top left: Former location of Women's City Club at 22 Park Avenue today. *Author photo.*

Former site of Todhunter School today. *Author photo.*

The Cosmopolitan Club. *Author photo.*

The Roosevelt Hotel. *Author photo.*

The lobby of 120 Broadway with its coffered ceiling and polished marble floors and walls was restored to its original appearance in the late 1980s. The building is a New York City landmark and also a National Historic Landmark.[360]

See chapter 9 for more details on FDR's business and legal career.

Former location of Women's City Club, 22 Park Avenue

The club, north of East 35th Street, was founded in 1915 by suffragists to pursue issues relating to women and children. Eleanor Roosevelt joined in 1923 and later chaired its city planning committee and served as first vice president. Now named Women Creating Change, the organization is still active in New York City.[361]

The Roosevelt Hotel, 45 East 45th Street

Named in honor of President Theodore Roosevelt, the hotel was developed by the New York Central Railroad and the New York, New Haven and Hartford Railroad. The nineteen-story structure east of Madison Avenue was designed by George B. Post & Son with an Italian Renaissance Revival–style façade. It opened on September 22, 1924, with more than one thousand rooms. It closed on December 18, 2020, due to financial losses associated with the COVID-19 pandemic. New York City reopened it as a shelter for asylum seekers in 2023, a use that was being phased out in 2025.[362]

Site of Todhunter School, 66 East 80th Street

The Todhunter School was a private college-preparatory school for upper-class girls founded by English-born Winifred Todhunter, a graduate of Oxford University. Eleanor Roosevelt's close friend Marion Dickerman taught there starting in 1922. In 1927, Dickerman, Eleanor and friend Nancy Cook purchased the school. Dickerman served as principal until 1937 while Eleanor spent time there as vice principal and teacher from 1927 to 1932. She remained associated with the school until 1938. The following year, the school merged with the Dalton School.[363]

Cosmopolitan Club, 122 East 66th Street

The club was established in 1909 and soon became a place where accomplished women in the arts and literature gathered to socialize and exchange ideas.

Eleanor Roosevelt was elected a member on February 2, 1927, and remained very active until her death in 1962, according to club librarian Declan Sokolska. Eleanor hosted many lunches and dinners and gave four lectures at the club. Other members have included Helen Hayes, Pearl Buck, Marian Anderson, Margaret Mead and Willa Cather.

The club has its roots in a decision in 1907 by a young mother named Ethel Hoyt to enlist the aid of two friends to establish the Club for Governesses in a furnished room in a kindergarten so their governesses would have a place to spend their limited leisure time. In 1909, the governesses and other "self-supporting professional women" moved their club, now called the Cosmos, to rooms on 33rd Street. By 1910, the club welcomed a wider mix of accomplished women, including nonprofessionals, to join a new Women's Cosmopolitan Club, soon shortened to the Cosmopolitan Club. Running out of space, in 1914 the club moved to a renovated church at Lexington Avenue and 40th Street. By the late 1920s, the club was again outgrowing its home. It acquired three properties, at 122–24 East 66th Street and 129 East 65th Street, in 1930 to build the current ten-story brick clubhouse with white marble trim and wrought-iron balconies.[364]

Boy Scouts Tablet, Prospect Park, Brooklyn

A bronze plaque was erected on a boulder at the top of Long Meadow in 1919. Its inscription reads, "In remembrance of Theodore Roosevelt/ The Boy Scouts of America of the Prospect Heights District planted these trees 1919."

Theodore Roosevelt Park, Columbus Avenue from 77th to 81st Streets and 77th and 81st Streets between Columbus Avenue and Central Park West

The American Museum of Natural History was constructed starting in 1929 in what was then named Manhattan Square. The narrow green space that remains of that park on the south, west and north sides of the museum was renamed for TR in 1958 to mark the centennial of his birth.

The Nobel Monument, an obelisk in the northwest section of the park, is inscribed with the names of American Nobel Prize winners, starting with Roosevelt's peace prize in 1906.

The Bull Moose Dog Run, named for TR's Progressive Party or Bull Moose campaign for president in 1912, is just west of the entrance to the Rose Center for Earth and Space on 81st Street.[365]

American Museum of Natural History's Theodore Roosevelt Memorial Building, Central Park West at 79th Street

The two-story building serves as New York State's official memorial to Theodore Roosevelt. It was designed by John Russell Pope, also the architect of the Jefferson Memorial and the West Building of the National Gallery of Art in Washington, D.C. TR spent much time at the museum during his childhood and contributed many specimens to its collections over his lifetime. The Theodore Roosevelt Memorial includes the museum's Central Park West entrance, the Theodore Roosevelt Memorial Hall and the Theodore Roosevelt Rotunda. The memorial, designed in the grand Roman style, was authorized by the New York State Legislature in 1924 and built between 1929 and 1935. The cornerstone was laid on October 27, 1931, by Franklin D. Roosevelt, Roosevelt's fifth cousin, who was governor at the time.

Bas-relief sculptures flanking the façade were created in 1936 by Edward Field Sanford Jr. and depict eighteen species of wild game. Above the columns along a parapet wall are four life-size sculptures of notable American explorers and naturalists Daniel Boone, John James Audubon, William Clark and Meriwether Lewis.

At the center of the rotunda, visitors can sit on a bench next to a bronze sculpture depicting Roosevelt during a famous 1903 camping trip to Yosemite with naturalist John Muir. It was created by Brooklyn's Studio EIS and installed in 2012.

In 1939, a bronze equestrian statue of Roosevelt by James Earle Fraser was installed in front of the building off Central Park West. Fraser (1876–1953) was a prominent American sculptor who designed numerous public monuments, including a bust of Roosevelt in the U.S. Senate. Fraser depicted TR flanked by standing allegorical figures representing Africa and America. The presence of those figures led to increasing criticism in recent years that the sculpture was racist. Protestors covered the base of the statue with red paint on the morning of October 26, 2017. In

Clockwise from top left: Theodore Roosevelt Park. *Author photo.*

Boy Scout monument in Prospect Park. *NYC Parks.*

Bull Moose Dog Run. *Author photo.*

Theodore Roosevelt Park Nobel Monument. *Author photo.*

Opposite: The American Museum of Natural History's Theodore Roosevelt Memorial Building. *Author photos.*

ROOSEVELT
MEMORIAL ★ HALL

MEDAL OF HONOR RECIPIENT
AUTHOR AND NATURALIST

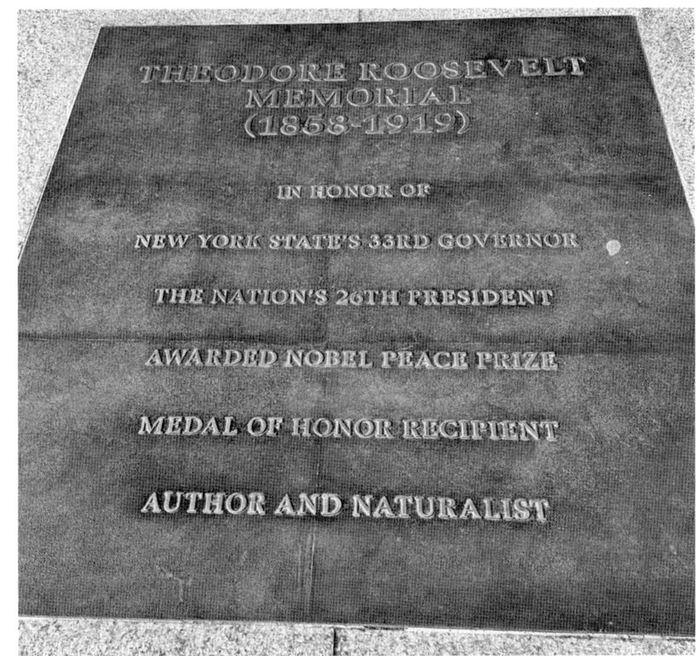
THEODORE ROOSEVELT
MEMORIAL
(1858-1919)
IN HONOR OF
NEW YORK STATE'S 33RD GOVERNOR
THE NATION'S 26TH PRESIDENT
AWARDED NOBEL PEACE PRIZE
MEDAL OF HONOR RECIPIENT
AUTHOR AND NATURALIST

2018, a commission appointed by New York City Mayor Bill de Blasio to review statues on city property made no recommendation to remove the TR sculpture. In July 2019, the museum opened an exhibit about it. Then on June 21, 2020, the museum announced it would remove the statue. Museum President Ellen V. Futter said the decision was based on the sculpture's "hierarchical composition." She told the staff that "many of us find its depictions of the Native American and African figures and their placement in the monument racist."

With the support of Roosevelt's descendants, on June 21, 2021, the New York City Public Design Commission voted unanimously to remove the statue and relocate it to an institution devoted to Roosevelt. On November 19, the Theodore Roosevelt Presidential Library Foundation announced it would accept the statue as a long-term loan for display at the Theodore Roosevelt Presidential Library scheduled to open in Medora, North Dakota, in 2026. On January 19, 2022, the statue was removed and sent to North Dakota, where it was placed in storage awaiting the opening of the library.[366]

Eleanor Roosevelt residence, 20 East 11th Street

While living in the White House, the first lady spent considerable time in Greenwich Village with Esther Lape and her partner Elizabeth Read while Franklin was often at Warm Springs seeking relief from polio. Lape and Read persuaded Eleanor to rent the third-floor apartment in their five-story brick building at 20 East 11th Street. She lived there from 1932 until 1942, as noted in a brass plaque near the door.[367]

Sara D. Roosevelt Park

The park, at East Houston Street to Canal Street between Chrystie Street and Forsyth Street, was created in 1934 on land that was originally purchased by Isaac Roosevelt in 1785. The dedication ceremony on September 14, 1934, was attended by 100,000 people and broadcast over the radio from Maine to Virginia. The largest stretch of open space in the Lower East Side neighborhood, the park includes the Golden Age Center for senior citizens, a recently renovated synthetic turf soccer field popular with local teenagers, several playgrounds, a vendors' market and a roller-skating rink.[368]

Eleanor and Franklin Roosevelt residence, 29 Washington Square West

After Sara Delano Roosevelt died in 1941 and with the twin townhouse on East 65th Street on the market, Franklin and Eleanor in 1942 signed a four-year lease for a seven-room apartment, 15A, at 29 Washington Square West, and Eleanor moved the family's New York City possessions there. Eleanor continued to live on Washington Square after FDR's death in April 1945 until 1949. See chapter 13.[369]

Former Hunter College Bronx Campus, 250 Bedford Park Boulevard West, the Bronx

The Bronx campus of Hunter College was established in 1931. In 1946, New York City officials offered the thirty-seven-acre site as a temporary home for the fledgling United Nations. From March 25 until August 15, the first American meetings of the Security Council were held in the gymnasium. Eleanor Roosevelt worked there on drafting the Universal Declaration of Human Rights after she was appointed by President Harry Truman to the U.S. delegation to the U.N.

In 1968, the school became an independent college in the City University of New York system. It was named after former New York governor, United States senator and philanthropist Herbert H. Lehman.[370] The gymnasium building now houses the college bookstore, Health and Wellness Center, Basic Needs Center and other departments.

Eleanor Roosevelt residence, the former Park Sheraton Hotel, 202 West 56th Street

By the end of 1949, Eleanor was renting suites in the Park Sheraton Hotel near 7th Avenue, where she enjoyed views of Central Park. After four years there, she decided she wanted her own home, and in 1953 she leased an apartment at 211 East 62nd Street. When her lease expired in 1958, Eleanor moved back to the Park Sheraton Hotel. See chapter 13.

Eleanor Roosevelt residence, 211 East 62nd Street

Eleanor lived at the Park Sheraton Hotel for four years before deciding she wanted her own home. So in 1953 she leased an apartment at 211

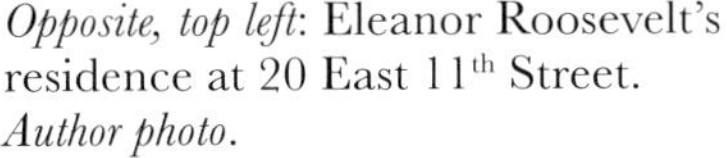

Opposite, top left: Eleanor Roosevelt's residence at 20 East 11th Street. *Author photo.*

Opposite, top rght: Former Eleanor and Franklin Roosevelt residence at 29 Washington Square West. *Author photo.*

Opposite, bottom: Sara D. Roosevelt Park. *Author photo.*

This page, clockwise from top left: The former Park Sheraton Hotel. *Author photo.*

The old gymnasium building at Herbert H. Lehman College, formerly the Bronx campus of Hunter College. *Lehman College photo.*

Eleanor Roosevelt's former residence at 211 East 62nd Street. *Author photo.*

East 62nd Street. Eleanor wrote about the move in her "My Day" column on August 31, 1953: "I have been in the Park Sheraton Hotel so long that I hated to tear myself away, but I think it will be better to have a little place where I can keep house and have my dogs in New York with me. I have a little garden, which should make a pleasant difference."[371]

Eleanor decorated her new home with a table whose base was a carved wooden elephant and four watercolors by her political advisor Louis Howe. Eleanor moved back to the Park Sheraton Hotel when her lease expired in 1958, See chapter 13.[372]

American Association for the United Nations, 45 East 65th Street and later in the Carnegie Endowment Building on East 46th Street

The organization was founded during World War II to generate support for creation of the United Nations. Eleanor Roosevelt completed her term as a U.S. representative to the United Nations General Assembly in 1953. The next year, she visited the association's New York office, which was located next to her former home on East 65" Street, and volunteered. She made personal appearances, led fundraising efforts and helped create chapters on college campuses and in communities across the country. The AAUN merged with the U.S. Committee for the United Nations in 1964 to form the United Nations Association of the United States of America. Eleanor Roosevelt remained involved with the organization until her death in 1962. It is now a program of the United Nations Foundation. See chapter 13.[373]

Eleanor Roosevelt's final residence, 55 East 74th Street

In 1958, Eleanor's friend Edna Gurewitsch, a successful art dealer who was the wife of her personal physician, David Gurewitsch, suggested what would become the former first lady's final residence in New York City. Edna asked Eleanor if she would be interested in sharing a townhouse with the couple. When Eleanor liked the idea, Edna searched the city for a property that would accommodate the three of them as well as her husband's practice.

Edna selected a townhouse at 55 East 74th Street. It was one of a group of eight similar buildings designed in 1889 by the architectural partnership of Buchman and Deisler. The neo-Renaissance building was fronted by

Greek columns with a sweeping curved staircase leading to the upper floors from the main entrance area's marble floor. Eleanor occupied the first three floors while writing for *McCall's* magazine, turning out her "My Day" column and using it as base for her extensive lecturing. The Gurewitsches were on the fourth and fifth floors.

Eleanor died in her bed at the townhouse on November 7, 1962. Over the years, the townhouse has had many subsequent owners. See chapter 13.[374]

Eleanor Roosevelt Memorial, Riverside Park

Eleanor Roosevelt is the only first lady honored with a statue in a New York City park, at Riverside Drive and 72nd Street. Her great-granddaughter was

Above: Eleanor Roosevelt statue in Riverside Park. *Author photo.*

Left: The exterior of Eleanor Roosevelt's final residence at 55 East 74th Street. *Author photo.*

the model for sculptor Penelope Jencks's 1996 work. The roundel reads: "Where, after all, do universal human rights begin? In small places, close to home. Such are the places where every man, woman and child seeks equal justice, equal opportunity, equal dignity. Eleanor Roosevelt, 1958."[375]

FRANKLIN DELANO ROOSEVELT FOUR FREEDOMS STATE PARK, ROOSEVELT ISLAND

The name of Welfare Island in the East River was changed to Roosevelt Island in 1973 with the idea of building an FDR memorial there. The memorial on four acres at the southern tip of the island was designed in 1974 by architect Louis Kahn to celebrate the four freedoms FDR articulated in his 1941 State of the Union address. They are freedom of conscience and religion; freedom of thought, belief, opinion and expression, including freedom of the press and other media of communication; freedom of peaceful assembly; and freedom of association.

Construction finally began on March 29, 2010, and was completed on budget and on schedule in September 2012.

The plaza features the words from FDR's speech on the granite walls and a six-foot-tall bronze bust of Roosevelt by Jo Davidson, originally sculpted in clay in 1933. The monument was dedicated on October 17, 2012, by President Bill Clinton, Governor Andrew Cuomo, Mayor Michael Bloomberg, and deputy U.S. Representative to the United Nations Willam vanden Heuvel, who was instrumental in creating the park. At the ceremony, the site was officially designated a New York State park by Cuomo. It opened to the public on October 24, 2012.[376]

Appendix B

TIMELINE OF ROOSEVELTS IN NEW YORK CITY

- The first Roosevelt in America, Claes Martenszen van Rosenvelt, arrives in New Amsterdam from Holland between 1644 and 1649.
- Cornelius Van Schaack Roosevelt, grandfather of President Theodore Roosevelt, is born on January 30, 1794.
- Robert B. Roosevelt, uncle of future president Theodore Roosevelt, is born in Manhattan on August 7, 1829.
- Theodore Roosevelt Sr., father of the future president, is born on September 22, 1831.
- Theodore Roosevelt's mother, Martha Stewart "Mittie" Bulloch Roosevelt, is born on July 8, 1835, in Hartford, Connecticut.
- Sara Delano Roosevelt, mother of future President Franklin D. Roosevelt, is born on September 21, 1854, at her family's estate, Algonac, near Newburgh.
- Anna "Bamie" Roosevelt, older sister of Theodore Roosevelt, is born on January 18, 1855.

- Theodore Roosevelt, the future president, is born on October 27, 1858, at 28 East 20th Street.

- Elliott Roosevelt, brother of Theodore Roosevelt, is born on February 28, 1860.

- Corinne Roosevelt, younger sister of Theodore Roosevelt, is born on September 27, 1861.

- Cornelius Van Schaack Roosevelt dies on July 17, 1871, in Oyster Bay.

- Theodore Roosevelt begins his studies at Harvard College in September 1876.

- Theodore Roosevelt Sr. dies at his West 57th Street home on February 9, 1878.

- In 1880, Theodore Roosevelt graduates from Harvard College and then marries Alice Hathaway Lee on October 27, 1880, his twenty-second birthday.

- Sara Delano at age twenty-six marries widower James Roosevelt, who is twice her age, on October 7, 1880.

- Theodore Roosevelt is elected to the New York Assembly in November 1881, the youngest person ever elected to that office.

- On January 30, 1882, Sara Delano Roosevelt gives birth to her only child, Franklin Delano Roosevelt, at Hyde Park.

- Corinne Roosevelt marries Douglas Robinson on April 29, 1882.

- Elliott Roosevelt, brother of Theodore Roosevelt and father of future First Lady Eleanor Roosevelt, becomes engaged to Anna Rebecca Hall on Memorial Day 1883, and the couple marries on December 1.

- Alice Lee Roosevelt, wife of Theodore Roosevelt, gives birth to daughter Alice on February 12, 1884.

- On February 14, Valentine's Day 1884, Theodore's mother, Mittie, dies at the family's West 57th Street home from typhoid fever. His wife Alice dies later the same day from a kidney ailment.

- Anna Eleanor Roosevelt, the future first lady, is born on October 11, 1884.

- After returning from ranching in the Dakota Territory and running unsuccessfully for mayor, Theodore Roosevelt secretly marries his second wife, Edith Carow, in London on December 2, 1886.

- Anna Roosevelt, mother of Eleanor Roosevelt, contracts diphtheria and dies at the age of twenty-nine on December 7, 1892.

- Elliott Roosevelt, the alcoholic father of Eleanor, dies on August 14, 1894, at age thirty-four after attempting suicide by jumping out of a window in Abingdon, Virginia.

- While in England in 1895, Theodore Roosevelt's sister Bamie marries divorced Rear Admiral William Sheffield Cowles.

- FDR enters Groton in 1896.

- FDR's father, James, dies on December 8, 1900, during Franklin's freshman year at Harvard.

- FDR receives his Harvard degree on June 24, 1903.

- FDR begins his studies at Columbia Law School in September 1904.

- Eleanor Roosevelt marries Franklin D. Roosevelt in New York City on March 17, 1905. Her uncle, President Theodore Roosevelt, gives away the bride.

- Robert B. Roosevelt, uncle of Theodore Roosevelt, dies at his Lotos Lake estate in Sayville, Long Island, at age seventy-six on June 14, 1906.

- After passing the bar exam in 1907, FDR is hired as a law clerk by Carter, Ledyard and Milburn.

- FDR is elected to New York State Senate in an upstate district in 1912.

- FDR becomes assistant secretary of the navy on March 17, 1913.

- FDR is nominated for vice president at the Democratic National Convention in San Francisco on July 6, 1920, on the ticket with James N. Cox. He resigns as assistant secretary of the navy on August 6. He and Cox are defeated on November 2.

- In January 1921, FDR returns to work in his law firm of Emmet, Marvin & Roosevelt and simultaneously becomes the vice president in charge of the New York office of the Fidelity and Deposit Company of Maryland.

- FDR is paralyzed by polio on August 10, 1921, on Campobello Island.

- FDR is elected governor of New York on November 6, 1928.

- Theodore Roosevelt's older sister, Anna "Bamie" Roosevelt Cowles, dies at her home in Farmington, Connecticut, on August 25, 1931.

- FDR is elected president on November 8, 1932, while living at East 65th Street townhouse.

- Corinne Roosevelt Robinson dies on February 17, 1933.

- FDR sells his townhouse on East 65th Street to Hunter College in 1942.

- Franklin Delano Roosevelt dies on April 12, 1945, at Warm Springs, Georgia.

- Eleanor Roosevelt is elected as the head of the United Nations human rights commission in 1946.

- Eleanor Roosevelt dies from tuberculosis at age seventy-eight on November 7, 1962.

- Franklin Delano Roosevelt Four Freedoms State Park on Roosevelt Island is dedicated on October 17, 2012.

NOTES

1. The Early Roosevelts in New York

1. Miller, *Theodore Roosevelt*, 25.
2. Harmond, "Robert Barnwell Roosevelt."
3. McCullough, *Mornings on Horseback*, 40; Collier, *Roosevelts*, 16.
4. Butler, *Roosevelt Homes*, 17; McCullough, *Mornings on Horseback*, 40; Collier, *Roosevelts*, 16.
5. Lash, *Eleanor and Franklin*, preface.
6. Collier, *Roosevelts*, 16.
7. Russell, *Life and Work*, 78–79.
8. Collier, *Roosevelts*, 17.
9. Lash, *Eleanor and Franklin*, preface.
10. Butler, *Roosevelt Homes*, 17.
11. Lash, *Eleanor and Franklin*, preface; Russell, *Life and Work*, 78–79.
12. Butler, *Roosevelt Homes*, 17–18; Collier, *Roosevelts*, 17.
13. Butler, *Roosevelt Homes*, 18.
14. Lash, *Eleanor and Franklin*, preface, 4; Michaelis, *Eleanor*, 6, 8.
15. Collier, *Roosevelts*, 28.
16. Dalton, *Theodore Roosevelt*, 16.
17. McCullough, *Mornings on Horseback*, 39.
18. McCullough, *Mornings on Horseback*, 24.
19. T. Roosevelt, *Autobiography*, 6.
20. Russell, *Life and Work*, 80–81.

21. Lewis, *Life of Theodore Roosevelt*, 26–27; McCullough, *Mornings on Horseback*, 38.
22. Lash, *Eleanor and Franklin*, preface, 4; Michaelis, *Eleanor*, 6, 8; Robinson, *My Brother*, 2; Morgan, *Theodore Roosevelt*, 4; McCullough, *Mornings on Horseback*, 24, 27, 118.
23. McCullough, *Mornings on Horseback*, 26–27.
24. Lash, *Eleanor and Franklin*, preface.

2. Theodore Roosevelt Sr.'s Wedding Present

25. McCullough, *Mornings on Horseback*, 40, 42.
26. Putnam, *Theodore Roosevelt*, 20; Miller, *Theodore Roosevelt*, 23.
27. McCullough, *Mornings on Horseback*, 20.
28. McCullough, *Mornings on Horseback*, 20.
29. T. Roosevelt, *Autobiography*, 5–6.
30. Lash, *Love, Eleanor*, 6.
31. McCullough, *Mornings on Horseback*, 22–23.
32. McCullough, *Mornings on Horseback*, 22–23, 40, 138.
33. Lash, *Eleanor and Franklin*, 4.
34. Putnam, *Theodore Roosevelt*, 21; Miller, *Theodore Roosevelt*, 28; "Anna Roosevelt Cowles," National Park Service [hereafter NPS], https://www.nps.gov.
35. Miller, *Theodore Roosevelt*, 29; McCullough, *Mornings on Horseback*, 45; Dalton, *Theodore Roosevelt*, 23.
36. Dalton, *Theodore Roosevelt*, 23.
37. McCullough, *Mornings on Horseback*, 19–20.
38. McCullough, *Mornings on Horseback*, 35.
39. Lash, *Eleanor and Franklin*, 4.
40. Robinson, *My Brother*, 9.
41. T. Roosevelt, *Autobiography*, 8–9.
42. Dalton, *Theodore Roosevelt*, 26.

3. Life at 28 East 20th Street

43. T. Roosevelt, *Autobiography*, 12.
44. T. Roosevelt, *Autobiography*, 13.
45. Lewis, *Life of Theodore Roosevelt*, 40.
46. McCullough, *Mornings on Horseback*, 136–37.
47. Lash, *Eleanor and Franklin*, 5–6; McCullough, *Mornings on Horseback*, 36–37; Collier, *Roosevelts*, 38.
48. Lash, *Eleanor and Franklin*, 4–5.
49. Dalton, *Theodore Roosevelt*, 26–27.
50. Dalton, *Theodore Roosevelt*, 27.
51. Robinson, *My Brother*, 20–21; Russell, *Life and Work*, 81–82; McCullough, *Mornings on Horseback*, 57–58, 63.
52. McCullough, *Mornings on Horseback*, 55–56; Collier, *Roosevelts*, 33; Miller, *Theodore Roosevelt*, 34.
53. McCullough, *Mornings on Horseback*, 59.
54. Lash, *Eleanor and Franklin*, 5–6; McCullough, *Mornings on Horseback*, 36–37, 64; Collier, *Roosevelts*, 38.
55. Lash, *Eleanor and Franklin*, 4.
56. Dalton, *Theodore Roosevelt*, 25.
57. McCullough, *Mornings on Horseback*, 65–67.
58. Dalton, *Theodore Roosevelt*, 25.
59. McCullough, *Mornings on Horseback*, 65–67.
60. T. Roosevelt, *Autobiography*, 11–12.
61. T. Roosevelt, *Autobiography*, 8.
62. T. Roosevelt, *Autobiography*, 8.
63. McCullough, *Mornings on Horseback*, 31.
64. Lewis, *Life of Theodore Roosevelt*, 33.
65. McCullough, *Mornings on Horseback*, 28–29.
66. Lash, *Eleanor and Franklin*, 5.
67. Robinson, *My Brother*, 3–4.
68. Robinson, *My Brother*, 4.
69. McCullough, *Mornings on Horseback*, 137–38.
70. Lash, *Eleanor and Franklin*, 5–6.
71. Quoted in Caroli, *Roosevelt Women*, 70.
72. Caroli, *Roosevelt Women*, 70.
73. McCullough, *Mornings on Horseback*, 33–35.
74. McCullough, *Mornings on Horseback*, 35.
75. McCullough, *Mornings on Horseback*, 114.

76. McCullough, *Mornings on Horseback*, 113.
77. Putnam, *Theodore Roosevelt*, 25–26.
78. T. Roosevelt, *Autobiography*, 13.
79. Robinson, *My Brother*, 1.
80. McCullough, *Mornings on Horseback*, 35–36; Miller, *Theodore Roosevelt*, 30–31; Dalton, *Theodore Roosevelt*, 36–37.
81. McCullough, *Mornings on Horseback*, 110–12.
82. McCullough, *Mornings on Horseback*, 112; Miller, *Theodore Roosevelt*, 49.
83. Lewis, *Life of Theodore Roosevelt*, 34.
84. T. Roosevelt, *Autobiography*, 14.
85. T. Roosevelt, *Autobiography*, 14.
86. Dalton, *Theodore Roosevelt*, 41.
87. McCullough, *Mornings on Horseback*, 35–36; Collier, *Roosevelts*, 37; Miller, *Theodore Roosevelt*, 40.
88. Robinson, *My Brother*, 2.
89. T. Roosevelt, *Autobiography*, 17.
90. Dalton, *Theodore Roosevelt*, 53; McCullough, *Mornings on Horseback*, 115, 117–18.
91. T. Roosevelt, *Autobiography*, 18.

4. Robert Barnwell Roosevelt: Black Sheep of the Family

92. McCullough, *Mornings on Horseback*, 21.
93. N. Roosevelt, *Front Row Seat*, 15.
94. *The Game Fish of The Northern States of the United States, and British Provinces* (1862), *Superior Fishing; or, The Striped Bass, Trout, and Black Bass of the Northern States* (1865), *Florida and the Game Water Birds* (1868), *The Game Birds of the Coasts and Lakes of the Northern States of America* (1869), *Five Acres Too Much* (1869), *Progressive Petticoats; Or, Dressed to Death. The Autobiography of a Married Man* (1871). *Fish Hatching and Fish Catching* (1879) and *Florida and the Game Water-Birds of the Atlantic Coast and the Lakes of the United States with a Full Account of the Sporting along our Seashores and Inland Waters, and Remarks on Breech-Loaders and Hammerless Guns* (1884).
95. "Robert B. Roosevelt," *Harper's Weekly*.
96. "The President's Uncle, *New York Times*, June 15, 1906.

97. "Robert Barnwell Roosevelt," Theodore Roosevelt Center, https://www.theodorerooseveltcenter.org.
98. "Robert Barnwell Roosevelt," Theodore Roosevelt Center.
99. N. Roosevelt, *Front Row Seat*, 16.
100. Bleyer, "Forgotten Roosevelt."
101. N. Roosevelt, *Front Row Seat*, 15.
102. N. Roosevelt, *Front Row Seat*, 15.
103. R. Roosevelt, *Superior Fishing*, 184–95.
104. Bleyer, "Forgotten Roosevelt"; Harmond, "Robert Barnwell Roosevelt."
105. N. Roosevelt, *Front Row Seat*, 15.
106. Harmond, "Robert Barnwell Roosevelt"; "Robert Barnwell Roosevelt," Theodore Roosevelt Center.
107. Bleyer, "Forgotten Roosevelt."
108. Bleyer, "Forgotten Roosevelt."
109. McCullough, *Mornings on Horseback*, 21; Collier, *Roosevelts*, 30; Bleyer, "Forgotten Roosevelt."
110. McCullough, *Mornings on Horseback*, 22.
111. McCullough, *Mornings on Horseback*, 22; Bleyer, "Forgotten Roosevelt"; Spinzia, "Those Other Roosevelts."
112. Spinzia, "Those Other Roosevelts."
113. T. Roosevelt, "Robert Barnwell Roosevelt's Illegitimate Progeny"; Beard and Hoff, "Roosevelt Family in America"; Spinzia, "Those Other Roosevelts."
114. T. Roosevelt, *Autobiography*, 12.
115. Bleyer, "Forgotten Roosevelt."
116. Bleyer, "Forgotten Roosevelt."
117. "President's Uncle"; "Robert Barnwell Roosevelt," Theodore Roosevelt Center.
118. McCullough, *Mornings on Horseback*, 149–150, 232; "President's Uncle."
119. R. Roosevelt, *Five Acres Too Much*, A2-xiii.
120. R. Roosevelt, *Five Acres Too Much*, A2-xiii.
121. R. Roosevelt, *Five Acres Too Much*, 148–53.
122. R. Roosevelt, *Five Acres Too Much*, 233–43, 252.
123. Bleyer, "Forgotten Roosevelt"; Spinzia, "Those Other Roosevelts."
124. Bleyer, "Forgotten Roosevelt."
125. Harmond, "Robert Barnwell Roosevelt."
126. N. Roosevelt, *Front Row Seat*, 15.

5. Theodore Sr. Moves the Family Uptown

127. McCullough, *Mornings on Horseback*, 127.
128. McCullough, *Mornings on Horseback*, 127.
129. Theodore Sr. letter to Bamie, September 24, 1873, Theodore Roosevelt Collection, Harvard University [hereafter TRC].
130. Theodore Sr. letters to Mittie, July 20 and September 21, 1873; Theodore Sr. letter to Bamie, September 24, 1873, TRC.
131. Theodore Sr. letter to Mittie, July 20, 1873, TRC.
132. Theodore Sr. letter to Bamie, June 29, 1873, TRC.
133. McCullough, *Mornings on Horseback*, 135.
134. Dalton, *Theodore Roosevelt*, 56.
135. McCullough, *Mornings on Horseback*, 135–36.
136. TRC.
137. McCullough, *Mornings on Horseback*, 135–36.
138. McCullough, *Mornings on Horseback*, 140.
139. Robinson, *My Brother*, 4.
140. Robinson, *My Brother*, 88.
141. Putnam, *Theodore Roosevelt*, 123, 125.
142. Lash, *Eleanor and Franklin*, 8–9.
143. McCullough, *Mornings on Horseback*, 141.
144. Morris, *Rise of Theodore Roosevelt*, 94; memorandum written by Elliott Roosevelt in the TRC.
145. Robinson, *My Brother*, 104.
146. McCullough, *Mornings on Horseback*, 183; Collier, *Roosevelts*, 47.
147. Robinson, *My Brother*, 104–5.
148. Theodore Roosevelt Papers, Library of Congress
149. Collier, *Roosevelts*, 48.
150. McCullough, *Mornings on Horseback*, 218–20, 223–24, 225–26, 231; Collier, *Roosevelts*, 55; Miller, *Theodore Roosevelt*, 106.
151. Collier, *Roosevelts*, 56; "Corinne Roosevelt Robinson," Theodore Roosevelt Center at Dickinson State University, https://www.theodorerooseveltcenter.org.
152. Theodore Roosevelt Papers, Library of Congress.
153. Theodore Roosevelt Papers, Library of Congress.
154. Robinson, *My Brother*, 119; "Theodore Roosevelt Timeline," Theodore Roosevelt National Park, https://www.nps.gov/.
155. Bleyer, *Sagamore Hill*, 23.

156. Theodore Roosevelt Papers, Library of Congress
157. Collier, *Roosevelts*, 62–63; Morris, *Rise of Theodore Roosevelt*, 232.
158. McCullough, *Mornings on Horseback*, 283.
159. Putnam, *Theodore Roosevelt*, 385; McCullough, *Mornings on Horseback*, 283.
160. Putnam, *Theodore Roosevelt*, 386.
161. Theodore Roosevelt Papers, Library of Congress.
162. Robinson, *My Brother*, 123.
163. Miller, *Theodore Roosevelt*, 156.
164. Miller, *Theodore Roosevelt*, 156–57.

6. The Later Homes of the Oyster Bay Roosevelts

165. Lash, *Eleanor and Franklin*, 11, 13; Lash, *Love, Eleanor*, 8.
166. Lash, *Eleanor and Franklin*, 14, 18, 20–21, 24–25, 28, 30, 32; Freedman, *Eleanor Roosevelt*, 12; Michaelis, *Eleanor*, 17.
167. Lash, *Eleanor and Franklin*, 21, 24–25, 28, 30, 32; Freedman, *Eleanor Roosevelt*, 12; Michaelis, *Eleanor*, 17.
168. E. Roosevelt, *Autobiography of Eleanor Roosevelt*, 6–8.
169. Freedman, *Eleanor Roosevelt*, 12.
170. E. Roosevelt, *Autobiography of Eleanor Roosevelt*, 10–11; Freedman, *Eleanor Roosevelt*, 12, 16.
171. Freedman, *Eleanor Roosevelt*, 12, 14; Michaelis, *Eleanor*, 33.
172. Michaelis, *Eleanor*, 33.
173. Michaelis, *Eleanor*, 35; "Elliott Roosevelt," National Park Service, https://www.nps.gov/.
174. Michaelis, *Eleanor*, 36.
175. E. Roosevelt, *Autobiography of Eleanor Roosevelt*, 20, 35, 37, 39; Lash, *Love, Eleanor*, 8, 39; Lash, *Eleanor and Franklin*, 101.
176. Teague, *Mrs. L.*, 151.
177. Caroli, *Roosevelt Women*, 80; "Anna Roosevelt Cowles," National Park Service, https://www.nps.gov/.
178. McCullough, *Mornings on Horseback*, 284, 286; Morris, *Rise of Theodore Roosevelt*, 248.
179. Collier, *Roosevelts*, 69, 73; Caroli, *Roosevelt Women*, 77.

7. The Resurrection of Theodore Roosevelt Birthplace

180. National Park Service, Sagamore Hill National Historic Site, THRB 4297, Box One, Folder 2.
181. National Park Service, Sagamore Hill National Historic Site, THRB 4297, Box One, Folders 4 and 5.
182. National Park Service, Sagamore Hill National Historic Site, THRB 4297, Box One, Folders 36 and 37.
183. National Park Service, Sagamore Hill National Historic Site, THRB 4297, Box 1, Folder 37.
184. National Park Service, Sagamore Hill National Historic Site, THRB 4297, Box 2, Folder 1.
185. National Park Service, Sagamore Hill National Historic Site, THRB 4297, Box One, Folders 8 and 9.
186. National Park Service, Sagamore Hill National Historic Site, THRB 4297, Box One, Folders 11 and 12.
187. National Park Service, Sagamore Hill National Historic Site, THRB 4297, Box One, Folder 15.
188. National Park Service, Sagamore Hill National Historic Site, THRB 4297, Box One, Folder 29.

8. The National Park Service Takes Over the Birthplace

189. Bleyer, *Sagamore Hill*, 110–14.

9. Sara, Franklin and Eleanor Roosevelt

190. Collier, *Roosevelts*, 53–54, 216.
191. Butler, *Roosevelt Homes*, 19–20, 22.
192. Caroli, *Roosevelt Women*, 207–11.
193. Caroli, *Roosevelt Women*, 211–12.
194. Caroli, *Roosevelt Women*, 213.

195. "James Roosevelt," National Park Service, https://www.nps.gov; Collier, *Roosevelts*, 50–51.
196. Teague, *Mrs. L.*, 156.
197. Lash, *Eleanor and Franklin*, 113–16; Michaelis, *Eleanor*, 61; McCullough, *Mornings on Horseback*, 226.
198. Caroli, *The Roosevelt Women*, 216.
199. Lash, *Eleanor and Franklin*, 116–17, 119; Michaelis, *Eleanor*, 68.
200. Lash, *Eleanor and Franklin*, 14, 18, 20–21, 24–25, 28, 30, 32; Freedman, *Eleanor Roosevelt*, 12; Michaelis, *Eleanor*, 17.
201. E. Roosevelt, *Autobiography of Eleanor Roosevelt*, 13, 19–20; Michaelis, *Eleanor*, 34.
202. Michaelis, *Eleanor*, 72–73.
203. E. Roosevelt, *Autobiography of Eleanor Roosevelt*, 20, 35, 37, 39; Lash, *Love, Eleanor*, 8, 39; Lash, *Eleanor and Franklin*, 101.
204. E. Roosevelt, *Autobiography of Eleanor Roosevelt*, 41.
205. E. Roosevelt, *Autobiography of Eleanor Roosevelt*, 41–42.
206. E. Roosevelt, *Autobiography of Eleanor Roosevelt*, 44.
207. E. Roosevelt, *Autobiography of Eleanor Roosevelt*, 39–40.
208. Lash, *Eleanor and Franklin*, 135, 137.
209. E. Roosevelt, *Autobiography of Eleanor Roosevelt*, 47.
210. Peyser and Dwyer, *Hissing Cousins*, 53–54.
211. E. Roosevelt, *Autobiography of Eleanor Roosevelt*, 49.
212. Teague, *Mrs. L.*, 156; Peyser and Dwyer, *Hissing Cousins*, 53–54. (This famous quote is often repeated inaccurately as "He wants to be the bride at every wedding, the corpse at every funeral and the baby at every christening.")
213. E. Roosevelt, *Autobiography of Eleanor Roosevelt*, 49.
214. E. Roosevelt, *Autobiography of Eleanor Roosevelt*, 50.
215. E. Roosevelt, *Autobiography of Eleanor Roosevelt*, 50–51, 55; Lash, *Eleanor and Franklin*, 145, 152.
216. E. Roosevelt, *Autobiography of Eleanor Roosevelt*, 56, 60.
217. Lash, *Eleanor and Franklin*, 152.

10. The Double Townhouse on East 65th Street

218. Michaelis, *Eleanor*, 89.
219. Michaelis, *Eleanor*, 89.
220. Michaelis, *Eleanor*, 89; Gardner, *Roosevelt House at Hunter College*, 26, 29.

221. Michaelis, *Eleanor*, 89.
222. E. Roosevelt, *Autobiography of Eleanor Roosevelt*, 60–61.
223. Lash, *Eleanor and Franklin*, 152.
224. E. Roosevelt, *Autobiography of Eleanor Roosevelt*, 60–61.
225. E. Roosevelt, *Autobiography of Eleanor Roosevelt*, 60–61.
226. Holzer, "Roosevelt House," 116–18.
227. E. Roosevelt, *Autobiography of Eleanor Roosevelt*, 60–61.
228. *Treasures of New York: Roosevelt House.*
229. Michaelis, *Eleanor*, 108–9.
230. Michaelis, *Eleanor*, 109.
231. Barron, "Remembering the House F.D.R. Built."
232. Michaelis, *Eleanor*, 109.
233. E. Roosevelt, *Autobiography of Eleanor Roosevelt*, 61.
234. Holzer, "Roosevelt House," 118.
235. Gardner, *Roosevelt House at Hunter College*, 32–33.
236. Michaelis, *Eleanor*, 110.
237. E. Roosevelt, *Autobiography of Eleanor Roosevelt*, 61.
238. E. Roosevelt, *Autobiography of Eleanor Roosevelt*, 63; Michaelis, *Eleanor*, 111.
239. Lash, *Eleanor and Franklin*, 163.

11. The Townhouse Becomes a Political Headquarters

240. Kinkead and Maloney, "Law Clerk."
241. E. Roosevelt, *Autobiography of Eleanor Roosevelt*, 63.
242. E. Roosevelt, *Autobiography of Eleanor Roosevelt*, 70–71.
243. Holzer, "Roosevelt House," 119; Gardner, *Roosevelt House at Hunter College*, 15, 34.
244. Michaelis, *Eleanor*, 142, 156, 159, 163–67.
245. Teague, *Mrs. L.*, 156–58.
246. Michaelis, *Eleanor*, 189, 199.
247. Michaelis, *Eleanor*, 199.
248. "Franklin Delano Roosevelt's Desk," Roosevelt House Public Policy Institute at Hunter College, https://www.rooseveltthouse.hunter.cuny.edu.
249. "Franklin Delano Roosevelt's Desk."
250. "Franklin Delano Roosevelt's Desk."
251. E. Roosevelt, *Autobiography of Eleanor Roosevelt*, 114–17.

252. "Franklin Delano Roosevelt's Desk."
253. Michaelis, *Eleanor*, 218.
254. Holzer, "Roosevelt House," 119.
255. Gardner, *Roosevelt House at Hunter College*, 39–40.
256. Holzer, "Roosevelt House," 119–20; Michaelis, *Eleanor*, 218, 229; E. Roosevelt, *Autobiography of Eleanor Roosevelt*, 117.
257. Boettiger, *Love in Shadow*, 89.
258. "The Algonac Diaries and a Delano Family Tragedy," *delanopaperproject, Tumblr*, https://www.tumblr.com/.
259. Michaelis, *Eleanor*, 232–33.
260. Schenkman, "Algonac."
261. Michaelis, *Eleanor*, 232–33.
262. E. Roosevelt, *Autobiography of Eleanor Roosevelt*, 118.
263. E. Roosevelt, *Autobiography of Eleanor Roosevelt*, 117–19.
264. E. Roosevelt, *Autobiography of Eleanor Roosevelt*, 119.
265. "Franklin Delano Roosevelt's Desk."
266. E. Roosevelt, *Autobiography of Eleanor Roosevelt*, 120.
267. Gardner, *Roosevelt House at Hunter College*, 41–42.
268. "Franklin Delano Roosevelt's Desk."
269. E. Roosevelt, *Autobiography of Eleanor Roosevelt*, 120.
270. Lash, *Eleanor and Franklin*, 276.
271. E. Roosevelt, *Autobiography of Eleanor Roosevelt*, 120, 122, 124–25; Michaelis, *Eleanor*, 228.
272. Holzer, "Roosevelt House," 120.
273. Holzer, "Roosevelt House," 120.
274. "Franklin Delano Roosevelt's Desk."
275. E. Roosevelt, *Autobiography of Eleanor Roosevelt*, 141–42.
276. E. Roosevelt, *Autobiography of Eleanor Roosevelt*, 144–45; Collier, *Roosevelts*, 271.
277. Collier, *Roosevelts*, 294; E. Roosevelt, *Autobiography of Eleanor Roosevelt*, 149, 151.
278. Holzer, "Roosevelt House," 120; Gardner, *Roosevelt House at Hunter College*, 33, 44–45.
279. E. Roosevelt, *Autobiography of Eleanor Roosevelt*, 161–63.
280. Holzer, "Roosevelt House," 121–22.
281. E. Roosevelt, *Autobiography of Eleanor Roosevelt*, 162.
282. Holzer, "Roosevelt House," 122.
283. E. Roosevelt, *Autobiography of Eleanor Roosevelt*, 163.
284. Holzer, "Roosevelt House," 123.

285. Perkins, *Roosevelt I Knew*, 9.
286. Perkins, *Roosevelt I Knew*, 150.
287. Perkins, *Roosevelt I Knew*, 150–52.
288. Gardner, *Roosevelt House at Hunter College*, 46.
289. Holzer, "Roosevelt House," 124–25.
290. "Roosevelt House: Saving a National Treasure for a New Generation, 1943–2023," Roosevelt House Public Policy Institute at Hunter College, https://www.roosevelthouse.hunter.cuny.edu; Butler, *Roosevelt Homes*, 35.
291. Gardner, *Roosevelt House at Hunter College*, 48.
292. Gardner, *Roosevelt House at Hunter College*, 48–49.
293. E. Roosevelt, *Autobiography of Eleanor Roosevelt*, 235.
294. Butler, *Roosevelt Homes*, 36.

12. Hunter College Acquires Roosevelt House

295. Gardner, *Roosevelt House at Hunter College*, 52, 73.
296. Holzer, "Roosevelt House," 126–28; Gardner, *"Forward-Looking Place."*
297. Gardner, *Roosevelt House at Hunter College*, 69.
298. Gardner, *Roosevelt House at Hunter College*, 69, 71.
299. Greene, "My Brush with History."
300. Gardner, *Roosevelt House at Hunter College*, 52.
301. Roosevelt House Collection, Hunter College Archives.
302. Gardner, *Roosevelt House at Hunter College*, 54.
303. Gardner, *Roosevelt House at Hunter College*, 54.
304. Holzer, "Roosevelt House," 130–31.
305. Gardner, *Roosevelt House at Hunter College*, 55.
306. Gardner, *Roosevelt House at Hunter College*, 57–58.
307. Gardner, *Roosevelt House at Hunter College*, 58.
308. Gardner, *Roosevelt House at Hunter College*, 58.
309. Holzer, "Roosevelt House," 132.
310. Holzer, "Roosevelt House," 131.
311. Holzer, "Roosevelt House," 132.
312. E. Roosevelt, "My Day: November 24, 1943."
313. E. Roosevelt, "My Day: December 1, 1943."
314. Gardner, *"Forward-Looking Place"*; Gardner, *Roosevelt House at Hunter College*, 53, 63–64.

315. Gardner, *"Forward-Looking Place."*
316. Holzer, "Roosevelt House," 133.
317. Gardner, *"Forward-Looking Place."*
318. Gardner, *"Forward-Looking Place."*
319. Gardner, *"Forward-Looking Place."*
320. Gardner, *"Forward-Looking Place."*
321. Gardner, *"Forward-Looking Place."*
322. Gardner, *"Forward-Looking Place."*
323. Gardner, *"Forward-Looking Place."*
324. Gardner, *"Forward-Looking Place."*
325. Holzer, "Roosevelt House," 133.
326. Gardner, *Roosevelt House at Hunter College*, 65.
327. Gardner, *"Forward-Looking Place."*
328. Gardner, *"Forward-Looking Place."*
329. Gardner, *Roosevelt House at Hunter College*, 66–67.
330. Gardner, *Roosevelt House at Hunter College*, 67.
331. Holzer, "Roosevelt House," 135–36.
332. Holzer, "Roosevelt House," 138.
333. "List of New York City Designated Landmarks in Manhattan from 59th to 110th Streets," Wikipedia, https://en.wikipedia.org.
334. National Register Database and Research, National Park Service, https://www.nps.gov.

13. ELEANOR ROOSEVELT ON HER OWN

335. Butler, *Roosevelt Homes*, 36.
336. "Women Who Shaped the Universal Declaration," United Nations, https://www.un.org.
337. E. Roosevelt, "My Day: August 31, 1953," https://www2.gwu.edu.
338. "United Nations Association of the United States of America," Wikipedia, https://en.wikipedia.org/.
339. Butler, *Roosevelt Homes*, 36.
340. Butler, *Roosevelt Homes*, 36–38, 40.
341. E. Roosevelt, "My Day: December 2, 1959," https://www2.gwu.edu.
342. Butler, *Roosevelt Homes*, 36–38, 40.

14. The Restoration of Roosevelt House

343. Gardner, *"Forward-Looking Place."*
344. Gardner, *"Forward-Looking Place."*
345. Gardner, *"Forward-Looking Place."*
346. Holzer, "Roosevelt House," 139.
347. Jennifer Raab, interview with the author, October 9, 2023.
348. Gardner, *"Forward-Looking Place."*
349. Holzer, "Roosevelt House," 139.
350. Holzer, "Roosevelt House," 139.
351. Holzer, "Roosevelt House," 139.
352. Holzer, "Roosevelt House," 131.
353. Gardner, *"Forward-Looking Place."*
354. Holzer, "Roosevelt House," 144.

Appendix A. Roosevelt-Related Sites in New York City

355. McCullough, *Mornings on Horseback*, 141; "Roosevelt House: Saving a National Treasure."
356. Butler, *Roosevelt Homes*, 19–20, 22.
357. "LPC Designates 7 Broadway Buildings South of Union Square as Individual Landmarks," NYC Landmarks Preservation Commission, https://www.nyc.gov.
358. "Webster Hotel," Wikipedia, https://en.wikipedia.org; "Club Quarters Hotel, Times Square–Midtown," Club Quarters, https://clubquartershotels.com.
359. "Franklin Delano Roosevelt's Desk."
360. "Franklin Delano Roosevelt's Desk."
361. "Women Creating Change," Wikipedia, https://en.wikipedia.org.
362. "Roosevelt Hotel (Manhattan)," Wikipedia, https://en.wikipedia.org.
363. Papers of Marion Dickerman.
364. "A Brief History of the Cosmopolitan Club," The Cosmopolitan Club, https://www.cosclub.com.
365. "Theodore Roosevelt Memorial," American Museum of History, https://www.amnh.org.

366. "Theodore Roosevelt Memorial"; "*Equestrian Statue of Theodore Roosevelt* (New York City)," Wikipedia, https://en.wikipedia.org.
367. Butler, *Roosevelt Homes*, 35.
368. "Sara D. Roosevelt Park," NYC Parks, https://www.nycgovparks.org.
369. Butler, *Roosevelt Homes*, 36.
370. "History of Lehman College," Legman College, https://lehman-undergraduate.catalog.cuny.edu.
371. E. Roosevelt, "My Day: August 31, 1953," https://www2.gwu.edu.
372. Butler, *Roosevelt Homes*, 36.
373. "United Nations Association of the United States of America," Wikipedia, https://en.wikipedia.org.
374. Butler, *Roosevelt Homes*, 36–38, 40.
375. Penelope Jencks Solo Exhibitions, http://www.penelopejencks.com/.
376. "The Park," Four Freedoms Park Conservancy, https://www.fdrfourfreedomspark.org.

BIBLIOGRAPHY

American Museum of Natural History. "Theodore Roosevelt Memorial." https://www.amnh.org.

Barron, James. "Remembering the House F.D.R. Built (Well, His Mother Did)." *New York Times*, November 29, 2018.

Beard, Timothy Field, and Henry B. Hoff. "The Roosevelt Family in America: A Genealogy." *Theodore Roosevelt Association Journal* 16, nos. 1–3 (Winter 1990).

Bleyer, Bill. "The Forgotten Roosevelt." *The Newsday Magazine*, October 6, 1985.

———. *Sagamore Hill*. The History Press, 2016.

Boettiger, John R. *A Love in Shadow*. W.W. Norton, 1978.

Butler, Susan. *Roosevelt Homes of the Hudson Valley: Hyde Park and Beyond*. The History Press, 2020.

Caroli, Betty Boyd. *The Roosevelt Women*. Basic Books, 1998.

Collier, Peter, with David Horowitz. *The Roosevelts: An American Saga*. Simon & Schuster, 1994.

Dalton, Kathleen. *Theodore Roosevelt: A Strenuous Life.* Alfred A. Knopf, 2002.

Frank Leslie's Illustrated Newspaper. "Hon. Robert B Roosevelt, United States Minister to the Netherlands." May 26, 1888.

Freedman, Russell. *Eleanor Roosevelt: A Life of Discovery.* Clarion Books, 1993.

Gardner, Deborah S. *"A Forward-Looking Place": Roosevelt House at 75 Years.* Exhibit at Roosevelt House, Hunter College, 2022.

———. *Roosevelt House at Hunter College: The Story of Franklin and Eleanor's New York City Home.* Lehman Institute of American History and Hunter College, The City University of New York, 2009.

———. "Roosevelt House: Saving a National Treasure for a New Generation, 1943–2023." Roosevelt House Public Policy Institute at Hunter College. https://www.roosevelthouse.hunter.cuny.edu.

Greene, Marion Shomer. "My Brush with History. Lonely (First) Lady." *American Heritage* 51 no. 6 (October 2000): 26.

Harmond, Richard P. "Robert Barnwell Roosevelt and the Early Conservation Movement," *Theodore Roosevelt Journal* 14, no. 2 (Summer 1988).

Harper's Weekly. "Robert B. Roosevelt." September 23, 1871.

Holzer, Harold. *The Presidents vs. the Press: The Endless Battle Between the White House and the Media—from the Founding Fathers to Fake News.* Dutton, 2020.

———. "Roosevelt House: Jewel in the Hunter Crown." In *Hunter 150*. Hunter College, 2020.

Kinkead, Eugene, and Russell Maloney. "Law Clerk." *The New Yorker*, April 13, 1945.

Lash, Joseph P. *Eleanor and Franklin.* W.W. Norton & Company, 1971.

———. *Love, Eleanor.* Doubleday & Company, 1982.

Lewis, William Draper. *The Life of Theodore Roosevelt.* United Publishers, 1919.

McCullough, David. *Mornings on Horseback: The Story of an Extraordinary Family, a Vanished Way of Life and the Unique Child Who Became Theodore Roosevelt.* Simon & Schuster, 1981.

Michaelis, David. *Eleanor.* Simon & Schuster, 2020.

Miller, Nathan. *Theodore Roosevelt: A Life.* William Morrow and Company, 1992.

Morgan, James. *Theodore Roosevelt: The Boy and the Man.* Grosset & Dunlap, 1919.

Morris, Edmund. *The Rise of Theodore Roosevelt.* Coward, McCann & Geoghegan Inc., 1979.

New York Times. "The President's Uncle, R.B. Roosevelt, Dead." June 15, 1906.

O'Keefe, Edward F. *The Loves of Theodore Roosevelt: The Women Who Created A President.* Simon & Schuster, 2024.

Papers of Marion Dickerman, 1918–1975. Franklin D. Roosevelt Presidential Library and Museum. https://www.fdrlibrary.org.

Perkins, Frances. *The Roosevelt I Knew.* Viking Press, 1946.

Peyser, Marc, and Timothy Dwyer. *Hissing Cousins.* Nan A. Talese/Doubleday, 2015.

Politico. "Eleanor Roosevelt Weds FDR, March 17, 1905." *This Day in Politics.* https://www.politico.com.

Pringle, Henry F. *Theodore Roosevelt: A Biography.* Harcourt, Brace and Company, 1931.

Putnam, Carlton. *Theodore Roosevelt*, vol. 1. *The Formative Years.* Charles Scribner's Sons, 1958.

Raab, Jennifer. Interview with the author. October 9, 2023.

Robinson, Corinne Roosevelt. *My Brother Theodore Roosevelt.* Charles Scribner's Sons, 1921.

Roosevelt, Eleanor. *The Autobiography of Eleanor Roosevelt.* Da Capo Press, 1992.

———. "My Day, November 24, 1943." *Eleanor Roosevelt Papers Digital Edition.* https://www2.gwu.edu.

———. "My Day, December 1, 1943." *Eleanor Roosevelt Papers Digital Edition.* https://www2.gwu.edu.

———. "My Day, August 31, 1953." *Eleanor Roosevelt Papers Digital Edition.* https://www2.gwu.edu.

Roosevelt, Nicholas. *A Front Row Seat.* University of Oklahoma Press, 1953.

Roosevelt, Robert B. *Five Acres Too Much.* Harper & Brothers, 1869.

———. *Progressive Petticoats; Or, Dressed to Death. The Autobiography of a Married Man.* G.W. Carleton & Company, 1871.

———. *Superior Fishing.* Carleton, 1865.

Roosevelt, Theodore. *An Autobiography.* Charles Scribner's Sons, 1920.

Roosevelt, Tweed. "Robert Barnwell Roosevelt's Illegitimate Progeny and the Extraordinary Massie Affair." *Theodore Roosevelt Association Journal* 35, no. 3 (Summer 2014).

Russell, Thomas H. *Life and Work of Theodore Roosevelt.* L.H. Walter, 1918.

Schenkman, A.J. "Algonac: The Delano's Hudson River Estate." New York Almanack, December 13, 2021. https://www.newyorkalmanack.com.

Spinzia, Raymond E. "Those Other Roosevelts: The Fortescues." The Oyster Bay Historical Society *Freeholder*, July 2010.

Teague, Michael. *Mrs. L: Conversations with Alice Roosevelt Longworth.* Gerald Ducksworth, 1981.

———. "Robert Barnwell Roosevelt." https://www.theodorerooseveltcenter.org.

Treasures of New York: Roosevelt House. PBS documentary, 2012.

INDEX

N

O

P

R

S

T

U

V

W

ABOUT THE AUTHOR

Audrey C. Tiernan, copyright 2016.

Bill Bleyer was a prize-winning staff reporter for *Newsday*, the Long Island daily newspaper, for thirty-three years before retiring in 2014 to write books and freelance for the newspaper and magazines.

He has written six previous books published by The History Press: *The Sinking of the Steamboat Lexington on Long Island Sound* (2023); *George Washington's Long Island Spy Ring: A History and Tour Guide* (2021); *Long Island and the Sea: A Maritime History* (2019); *Fire Island Lighthouse: Long Island's Welcoming Beacon* (2017); *Sagamore Hill: Theodore Roosevelt's Summer White House* (2016); and, with coauthor Harrison Hunt, *Long Island and the Civil* War (2015).

His work has been published on Smithsonian.com and in *Civil War News*, *America's Civil War*, *Naval History*, *Sea History*, *Lighthouse Digest* and numerous other magazines and newspapers.

Prior to joining *Newsday*, Bleyer worked at *The Courier-News* in Bridgewater, New Jersey, as a reporter and editor. He began his career as editor of the *Oyster Bay Guardian*.

Bleyer graduated Phi Beta Kappa with highest honors in economics from Hofstra University, where he has been an adjunct professor teaching journalism and economics. He has also been an adjunct professor and lecturer teaching Long Island maritime history at Webb Institute, the naval architecture college in Glen Cove, New York. He earned a master's degree in urban studies at Queens College of the City University of New York.

He lives in Bayville, Long Island.